ALTERATIONS AND ADAPTATIONS
OF SHAKESPEARE

AMS PRESS
NEW YORK

ALTERATIONS AND ADAPTATIONS OF SHAKESPEARE

By
FREDERICK W. KILBOURNE, Ph.D.

THE POET LORE COMPANY
Publishers, Boston
1906

Library of Congress Cataloging in Publication Data

Kilbourne, Frederick Wilkinson, 1872-
    Alterations and adaptations of Shakespeare.

    1. Shakespeare, William, 1564-1616--Adaptations.
I. Title.
PR2880.A1K5   1973   822.3'3   79-171065
ISBN 0-404-03674-0

Reprinted from an original in the collections of The Wilbur L. Cross Library, University of Connecticut

From the edition of 1906, Boston
First AMS edition published in 1973
Manufactured in the United States of America

AMS PRESS INC.
NEW YORK, N.Y. 10003

CONTENTS

I

	Page
Chapter One—General Discussion . . .	5

II

Chapter Two—The Tempest—The Two Gentlemen of Verona—The Merry Wives of Windsor	27
Chapter Three—Measure for Measure—The Comedy of Errors—Much Ado about Nothing—Love's Labour's Lost .	46
Chapter Four—A Midsummer Night's Dream—The Merchant of Venice—As You Like It—The Taming of the Shrew . .	65
Chapter Five—All's Well that Ends Well—Twelfth Night—The Winter's Tale—King John—Richard II—1 Henry IV—2 Henry IV	84
Chapter Six—Henry V—1, 2, and 3 Henry VI—Richard III—Henry VIII—Troilus and Cressida	101

CONTENTS—Continued

Chapter Seven—Coriolanus—Titus Andronicus—Romeo and Juliet—Timon of Athens 120

Chapter Eight—Julius Cæsar—Macbeth—Hamlet—King Lear—Othello . . 142

Chapter Nine—Antony and Cleopatra—Cymbeline—Pericles 173

III

Epilogue 187

I

GENERAL DISCUSSION

CHAPTER I. GENERAL DISCUSSION

ALL students of English literature are familiar with the fact that for a long period, beginning with the Restoration and practically ending with the eighteenth century, Shakespeare's plays were usually not represented in their unsophisticated forms but in altered or adapted ones conforming to the changed taste of the time.

A few of the more noteworthy of these revisions are known to such students and may have been read or glanced over by them, but general knowledge rarely goes beyond such facts as that Tate gave "Lear" a happy ending or that Cibber is responsible for certain phrases, as the well-known "Richard's himself again," which are still heard when "Richard the Third" is played and which are sometimes popularly attributed to Shakespeare. Even professed Shakespeare students, however, know little or nothing of the great body of these versions, which in the eighteenth century nearly or quite displaced the original plays — how extensively is testified by the interesting fact that the author of *The Tatler,* having occasion to quote from "Macbeth," quotes not from the original but from the D'Avenant alteration, apparently for the reason that its diction was the one that would be recognized by his readers or possibly because it was the one most familiar to himself.

It is my purpose to give in the ensuing pages the results of a study of these alterations and adaptations,

6 ALTERATIONS AND ADAPTATIONS

which was as thorough as I was able to make it, with so much of the material inaccessible.

Preliminarily, I shall notice the pronounced change in dramatic taste which differentiates the period I am dealing with from the preceding one, and then indicate the effect of the belief in different dramatic tenets on the opinion of Shakespeare. Thence I shall pass to a discussion of the principles of the dramatic art which came to rule and to which the playwrights of the time endeavored to make Shakespeare's plays conform by means of alteration. This done, I shall devote the bulk of the work to a more or less detailed description of the various altered versions and to comment on the individual modifications made, whether these changes were in the direction of the practical application of the special dramatic theories held or in that of the manifestation, not of any particular dramatic notion, but of the personal opinions, judgment, or caprice of a reviser.

With the closing of the theatres by Parliamentary ordinance in 1642, the old, or Elizabethan, drama, which had long been undergoing decay, came abruptly to an end. After the theatres were again thrown open at the Restoration a complete change of taste was soon evident. The masses were no longer attracted to the stage as in the previous period. The drama was dominated by the influence of the court and people of fashion and so it ceased to reflect the life of the nation. The spirit of the age was frivolous and, as Ward says, it "sought in the drama a mere stimulant of passion and satisfaction of curiosity."

Although the Restoration drama may be called the child of the old age of the Elizabethan, it was, however, a child brought up in a foreign country.

It was natural enough that a king and nobility who had been exiles in France should endeavor after their return to their native land to transplant many of the ideas acquired during their absence. This was done, and in no literary domain was the French influence more felt than in that of the drama. The dramatic principles employed by Corneille, Molière, and Racine came to be imposed upon the English drama, which, except in a few instances, as in Jonson's plays and some of the early dramas on classical models, had hitherto been free and untrammeled. Accordingly, the new plays began to conform more or less strictly to certain so-called rules of art based on Aristotle and others of the ancients and modified by French ideas and usages. As any notice of the original plays of the period, however, would not only be superfluous — they have already been abundantly discussed by other and abler students — but also foreign to my purpose, I shall pass without further delay to that with which I am chiefly concerned, the effect of this new taste on Shakespeare, as shown in the current opinions regarding him and also in the alterations of his plays which were the concrete manifestations of these opinions.

The plays of Shakespeare were not banished from the stage after the Restoration but continued to be acted with great success as they were especial favorites with the common people. The chief cause of their retention, however, seems to have been that their strong characters and striking situations furnished such great opportunities for histrionic and scenic effects. But the attitude of the people of fashion toward the plays was greatly different from that of the masses. The courtiers looked upon them as inferior works and did not disguise their contempt for them.

8   ALTERATIONS AND ADAPTATIONS

Two passages from Pepys will show this conclusively. Under the date of 1662, he says, "To the King's Theatre, where we saw 'Midsummer Night's Dream,' which I had never seen before, nor shall ever see again, for it is the most insipid, ridiculous play that ever I saw in my life;" and again, in 1666, he writes, "To Deptford by water, reading 'Othello, Moor of Venice,' which I ever heretofore esteemed a mighty good play; but, having so lately read 'The Adventures of Five Hours,' it seems a mean thing." When we are informed that the play which Pepys preferred to "Othello" had a variety of plots and intrigues, we may see to what extent the dramatic taste of the people of fashion had become degenerate, for these opinions of the gossipy Secretary to the Admiralty doubtless reflect the sentiment of many a courtier toward Shakespeare.

The attitude of the professional critics and literary men was also very unfavorable. It might be described as lukewarm admiration often tempered with open or thinly veiled disdain. Dryden, the greatest genius and the literary dictator of his time, had a great veneration for Shakespeare, yet his better judgment was often held in subjection to the depraved taste of those about him. He did not hesitate to break a lance with Shakespeare by writing a play on the same subject and, what was even more fatuous on his part, attempted to improve two of the great dramatist's best plays. The original work and the revisions were about equally damaging to their author's reputation for literary taste and judgment. He did not understand the real nature of the romantic drama, and moreover his employment as a hack writer made him, doubtless not unwillingly, follow the prevailing literary fashions. As Dryden grew older his appreciation of Shakespeare increased and his more mature criticisms show much less of the depreciative opinions expressed in his earlier prefaces and other critical articles. Still he found many faults in Shakespeare which he charitably attributed to that author's living in a less refined age.

The criticisms made by Dryden were repeated, with slight variations, by critics, dramatists, and editors down to the beginning of the nineteenth century. Passing by the absurd strictures of Rymer and Mrs. Lennox, the latter of whom denied Shakespeare any excellence, one may call to mind the criticisms of John Dennis and Charles Gildon, both of whom, as did Dryden, replied to Rymer in defense of Shakespeare, and the prefaces of Rowe, Pope, and lastly Doctor Johnson, who was almost frightened at his own temerity in justifying Shakespeare's rejection of the unities. These all recognized the genius of the great Elizabethan, but seemed to think that he worked without any method at all and lamented that he was unlearned and ignorant of the " rules of art." Not until the time of Coleridge were these false notions entirely eradicated.

Before considering what these rules of art were, for the observance of which the critics clamored, I must turn aside to notice one innovation which, as applied to Shakespeare's plays, had in many instances a damaging effect on them. As is well known, the stage furnishings in the Elizabethan period were severely simple — there was no movable scenery. After the introduction of that accessory, which, when kept in proper subordination, is a decided and welcome addition to the representation of a play, there was afforded great opportunity for scenic display, and some of the earlier alterations of the plays arose out of efforts made to produce elaborate effects of this kind. The plays of Shakespeare in their original form, or nearly so, were better acted by the company of which Betterton was the head; so Sir William D'Avenant, master of the rival company (the Duke's), to make head against the success of the King's Company, was, according to Cibber, " forced to add spectacle and music to action; and to introduce a new species of plays, since called dramatic operas, — all set off with the most expensive decorations of scenes and habits, with the best voices and dancers." Among others, D'Avenant chose two of Shakespeare's plays to be thus represented, namely, " The Tempest " and " Macbeth," which besides were materially altered as to plot. The new taste in this way established had some influence, for Shadwell turned " The Tempest " into a regular opera, as did also Garrick, and operatic additions were made to several of the other plays with the result in every case of badly disfiguring them, and, further, there has survived a tendency to make music and spectacle, especially the latter, prominent in Shakespearean representations. On the whole, however, this influence was comparatively unimportant, being confined to a few plays only. Most of the alterations were due to other causes to a consideration of which I shall now turn my attention.

I have mentioned that it was the universal opinion that, owing to his having lived in a barbarous age — that is, from the eighteenth-century point of view — and his own lack of education, Shakespeare was ignorant of the " rules of art." What were these " rules of art "? First in importance were the so-called Aristotelian unities of time and place, which had governed the classical drama and which had been imposed upon the French pseudo-classical drama by Corneille. With regard to the unity of action, it may be said, in passing, that there was never, even among the romanticists, any serious question as to the propriety of observing it, allowance being made for individual interpretation and application of the principle, and that, although changes were sometimes made by the alterers of Shakespeare to bring a play into what was regarded as closer conformity to it, it is not its violation but that of the other unities which was chiefly censured. So, when the unities are mentioned or referred to, it is to be understood that, unless otherwise indicated, those of time and place are meant. It will not be necessary to explain or to refute these principles here. They are well known and, among others, Doctor Johnson, in the preface to his edition of Shakespeare, has, not however without some misgiving, proved that the necessity for their observance rests upon false assumptions. It is no more binding upon an Englishman to observe them than for him to obey the laws of Draco. The romantic drama, the cardinal principle of which was absolute freedom of treatment in dramatizing a story, rejected them almost entirely. But to an age which derived its ideas of the drama from Corneille, Molière, and Racine, it seemed rank heresy or gross ignorance in an author not to make his plays "regular." The dramatists of the time, therefore, in their own plays, if not adhering strictly to the unities, at least observed them as nearly as possible. We do not object greatly to their doing this in the case of their own works, although by so doing they restricted the extent of the drama and lessened its variety and thus injured their own product; but when they called Shakespeare a barbarian because he designedly and deliberately neglected to observe these artificial rules, of which he was not, as they wrongly supposed, ignorant, and, what was far worse, considered themselves privileged to alter his plays at will to make them conform to these false principles, we cannot but condemn their mistaken efforts and deplore their ignorance and lack of reverence for the great master.

I have found but one attempt to give a play of Shakespeare's a strictly classical form, namely, the Duke of Buckinghamshire's treatment of "Julius Cæsar," in which the endeavor almost precisely to observe the unities caused the reviser to divide the play into two tragedies, in doing which he mutilated the text and was guilty of some absurdities. But all through the eighteenth century will be found, in connection with the other revisions, numerous changes to make the plays approach more nearly to conformity to the unities. Sometimes the desire to observe more closely the unity of action probably led, partly at least, to the omission of the comic underplot, or of the less important characters, or of some of the episodes, in every case to the detriment of the play so treated. Often the time of the action was restricted and large portions of a play omitted in consequence, the omissions being replaced by passages of the reviser's own composition. Again the would-be improvers overcame the objectionable (to them) shifting of the scene from place to place by confining it to one place or fewer places.

Another "rule of art" which the critics and dramatists considered necessary to be observed was that of poetical justice. According to this rule the virtuous should retire at the end of the play, as Doctor Johnson said of Tate's Cordelia, "with victory and felicity," while the wicked should receive the punishment they have merited. This idea needs no other refutation than that it is contrary to human experience. Even such a classicist as Addison saw the falsity of it and condemned it as a "chimerical notion." But his is an example of a better taste than is to be found in other critics of the period. Of course Shakespeare had violated this rule many times. Hear Dennis on this point: "The good and the bad perishing promiscuously in the best of Shakespeare's tragedies, there can be either none or very weak instruction in them." In this spirit Dryden set to work to remodel "Troilus and Cressida"; Tate, as we all know, gave "Lear," and James Howard, "Romeo and Juliet," a happy ending; and Dennis himself punished Aufidius in his version of "Coriolanus." These, however, are only some of the more important instances in which this rule was applied, there being numerous other minor cases which make it on the whole one of the most pernicious in its influence on the plays.

Another rule the observance of which Dryden and others regarded as essential was that the hero and heroine should not be villains. Dryden's opinion on this point, which he derived from Aristotle, is this: "It is absolutely necessary to make a man virtuous if we desire he should be pitied. We lament not, but detest, a wicked man; we are glad when we behold his crimes are punished and that poetical justice is done upon him. It is necessary that the hero of the play be not a villain, that is, the characters which should move our pity ought to have virtuous inclinations and degrees of moral goodness in them. As for a perfect character of virtue, it never was in nature, and therefore there can be no imitation of it;

14 ALTERATIONS AND ADAPTATIONS

but there are allays [alloys] of frailty to be allowed for the chief persons, yet so that the good which is in them shall outweigh the bad, and consequently leave room for punishment on the one side, and pity on the other." As Shakespeare had often gone counter to this theory, Dryden, to give an example of its practical application, and to show what Shakespeare should have done, altered the play in the preface to which this criticism is given in such a way as to make the heroine, Cressida, virtuous. This rule, besides being, as Scott says, "too nice and fastidious," is likewise not always true to experience. It would exclude such plays as "Richard III" and "Macbeth," and, moreover, the character of a villain may be so portrayed as to excite our pity or sympathy, as, for example, that of Shylock.

Another feature of the Elizabethan drama in general and Shakespeare in particular that gave offense to the classicists was the mingling of the tragic and the comic in the same play. That tragedy should be unrelieved by any particle of humor and that comedy should be all comic, was the doctrine in its unalloyed form, to which a playwright of pure taste must, in the opinion of true-blue classicists, conform strictly. Such extremists reprobated tragi-comedy altogether. Especially was the introduction of comic characters or scenes into tragedy reprehensible. "There is no place in tragedy," said Gildon, "for anything but grave and serious actions." They did not perceive that this is not so in life and that Shakespeare, whom they charged with deficiency or barbarity of taste for going counter to this "rule of art," was familiar with the doctrine (it had been put forth and followed before his time), had seen its falsity, and had deliberately rejected it.

The practice of the sticklers for art fell short, however, of their theory. The introduction of tragic scenes into comedy was not so much objected to as the reverse procedure, and tragi-comedy came to be, because of its popularity, a more or less accepted kind of drama, being regarded as a sort of concession to human weakness. Dryden apologetically took its part and, later, Doctor Johnson came to its defense. But the strict classicists clung desperately to the idea that no comedy should be permitted in a tragedy; the comic portions were thought to counteract the effect of the tragic instead of to heighten it, as we know it to do, and as Shakespeare, as a real dramatic artist, had clearly perceived. To be sure, it came to pass that, among the less rigid holders of the theory we are discussing, a tragedy, even when altered to have a happy ending, as Tate's "Lear" or Howard's "Romeo and Juliet," was still a tragedy, provided there was sufficient of the tragic element in the play, but this belief savored of heresy. Shakespeare was censured greatly because of his practice as to this mingling of the tragic and the comic, and his introduction of low characters, nonsense, and buffoonery into his tragedies was regarded as disgracing them. This was the belief of Milton and especially of Voltaire. Of the attempt to improve Shakespeare in this respect we find many instances. This notion is responsible, for example, for the omission of the porter scene in "Macbeth" by D'Avenant, of the gravediggers in "Hamlet" by Garrick, and of the fool in "Lear" by Tate and his successors; and, in large measure, for the rejection of the comic characters and the comic underplots in such plays as Sheffield's "Julius Cæsar," D'Avenant's alteration of "Measure for Measure" ("The Law against Lovers"), and Gildon's revision of the same play, and Johnson's "Love in a Forest" ("As You Like It"). Rarely, alterers allowed their desire to display their own excellence in comic writing and to please the people, to go against their dramatic faith, for Tate added comedy to "Richard II," and Dennis, although censuring Shakespeare's practice, did likewise in the case of "Coriolanus." Thus, by their adherence to a false principle of art and by their doing violence to Shakespeare as a result of their mistaken belief, did the playwrights and critics exhibit most effectively their own lack of comprehension.

I come now to describe a practice affecting the plots of the plays that has been, perhaps, greater cause of their mutilation than has the application of any of the foregoing opinions. The dramatists of the eighteenth century believed that it was the business of a play to deal with the passion of love. There must be plenty of intrigue, or, at least, women must figure conspicuously in a play, otherwise the drama was not a true play. This idea was French in its origin, as may be seen from what Edward Phillips, the disciple of Milton, says of Corneille's practice in this respect: "Corneille, the great dramatic writer of France, wonderfully applauded by the present age, both among his own countrymen and our Frenchly-affected English, for the amorous intrigues, which if not there before, he commonly thrusts into his tragedies and acted histories; the imitation whereof among us, hath of late very much corrupted our English stage."

But not only did the dramatists adopt this device for their own works, but also they had the audacity to thrust "amorous intrigues," love affairs, and the like, into Shakespeare's tragedies and histories. The passion of misanthropy was not sufficient to be the subject of a tragedy like "Timon," but the drama must be "made into a play" by Shadwell, who gave Timon a couple of mistresses and omitted much of the original play to make room for a number of love scenes. Tate felicitates himself upon his hitting upon the expedient of introducing into "Lear" a love affair between Edgar and Cordelia, "to rectify what was wanting in the regularity and probability of the tale." Not content with that, he makes Edmund have a desire for her and amplifies on his criminal commerce with Goneril and Regan. Sheffield added love scenes to his alteration of "Julius Cæsar." But this Frenchified refinement was most extensively employed in the remodeling of the histories. These especially were considered not true plays because they did not answer to the definition of a tragedy or comedy. Nevertheless, although they could not of course be circumscribed by the unities, or at most only partly, it was the notion that they could be made more like plays than Shakespeare had left them. So they were remodeled by cutting out some of the scenes and substituting for the omissions scenes of love intrigue and the like, which produced shameful mutilations.

How much greater knowledge of dramatic art and life Shakespeare shows in not thus limiting his subjects to one passion! As Doctor Johnson says, "He knew that any other passion, as it was regular or exorbitant, was a cause of happiness or calamity."

One or two minor theories that were held or practices that were followed, which had a slight influence on the alteration of Shakespeare's plays, remain to be mentioned and disposed of. It was a belief that tragedy should be confined as far as possible to royalty and persons of high position, and that a monarch, when the chief character of a tragedy, should be estimable. The former idea may have been responsible partly for the omission of comic characters in the tragedies and histories, and the latter in one case at least, namely, in Tate's "Richard II," was so applied as to make a weak monarch more worthy of the passive obedience that was his due. Again, we find that the desire for scenes of violence exercised some effect, for, besides usually retaining Shakespeare's scenes of this kind, the revisers frequently added to the number of them. This feature appears most pronouncedly in Tate's "Coriolanus," and in Ravenscroft's "Titus Andronicus," but there are several other plays that also exhibit it, as Durfey's "Cymbeline," in which an episode of putting out eyes is inserted.

It has been shown that the plays were altered in order to make them conform as much as possible to certain rules foreign to the spirit and practice of the romantic drama, namely, the unities, poetical justice, the rule that the chief characters of a play should be virtuous, and the rule that tragedy and comedy should not be mingled; that they were modified to admit music and spectacle, and sometimes to increase the number of scenes of violence; and, further, that they were altered to obey a rule derived from the French, which required the passion of love to figure prominently in every play. By far the greater number of the revisions were made in the interest of these false principles, but there are, however, a number that cannot be assigned to any of these causes. Some were made apparently with the object of improving the characterizations, and without exception failed of their purpose. Sometimes the histories were so altered as to emphasize a political doctrine or to serve as a medium for religious invective, instances of which kind are, however, fortunately few. Again, as in the D'Avenant alterations, changes were made to suit certain hastily conceived and bad theories of dramatic art.

It was a far too common practice to turn to Shakespeare for an afterpiece. Several plays were cut down by Garrick and others for this purpose, or parts of plays were so used. This reprehensible practice was doubtless resorted to because authors lacked subjects for such pieces, or because their invention was barren and they knew that there was abundance of material in Shakespeare's comedies. Several curious alterations, as, for example, James Miller's "Universal Passion" and Lacy's "Sauny the Scot," were undertaken with no apparent purpose other than to provide partly new plays.

In all these "versions," which were "perversions" and "adaptations which were a compound of mutilations and Procrustean extensions," there was exhibited not only the utmost lack of real dramatic art, but also the absence of any true reverence for the great dramatist, whose work, as has been said, the would-be improvers considered themselves at liberty not merely to omit, but to alter, add to, and otherwise mutilate at pleasure.

One more phase of this subject calls for notice before proceeding further, and that is the treatment of Shakespeare's diction by his adapters and revisers. The notion was held by an age whose own vocabulary was impoverished that Shakespeare's style was obsolete and needed refining. In the preface to his "Troilus and Cressida," which I have quoted from before in another connection, Dryden complained that many of Shakespeare's phrases were ungrammatical and coarse and that his style was affected and obscure because of the abundance of figurative expressions. So one finds him and others attempting to refine Shakespeare's style by substituting more modern equivalents for supposedly obsolete words (many of which are now in good usage), by removing the metaphorical expressions, and by making absolutely unnecessary and unwarrantable changes merely out of caprice. Verse was sometimes turned into prose, or *vice versa,* but there was no uniformity of practice in this. Again, the poetasters omitted many of Shakespeare's fine passages to make room for their own miserable stuff.

It might have been expected that some of the plays would in revision have been given the form of an heroic play in rime, but no one appears to have been bold enough or foolish enough to attempt this. It might have been done had that species of play had a longer vogue, but the attack on that dramatic *genre* by Buckingham in "The Rehearsal" and the abandonment of the use of rime by Dryden, which put an end to this short-lived type, doubtless prevented any of Shakespeare's plays being thus treated.

After reading these *rifacimenti* one is at a loss many times which to condemn the more, the changes in the plots or in the phraseology. No one who has not read such plays, for example, as D'Avenant's "Macbeth" or Granville's "Jew of Venice," can have any adequate conception of the unnecessary and wanton changes of words, expressions, lines, and passages. On the whole it is better to make no distinction in degree between the condemnation to be given to the treatment of plot and that called for by the treatment of diction. Almost without exception both are equally deserving of contempt and execration.

There is yet another very common practice that

calls for anything but commendation, and that is, the borrowing of passages from some other play or plays of Shakespeare, and even from plays of other authors, to eke out the dialogue of an altered version. It was reprehensible not only because unnecessary, but also because the passages chosen are often unsuited to the play or characters to which they are transferred.

It may be well at this point to answer the question that may arise, if in any cases improvements were made by the revisers? This may be answered in the affirmative, for in a number of instances minor changes were made for the better. It is conceivable that a playwright, working in a true spirit of reverence for Shakespeare and with a knowledge of the principles by which he was guided, could improve the plays in numerous instances, for Shakespeare is far from impeccable — "The only impeccable writers," says Hazlitt, "are those who never wrote." The proper way in which to alter Shakespeare is to make such omissions, transpositions, and other slight changes as are necessary, and many of the later acting versions, made in this spirit, have certainly improved the plays for representation. There is nothing wrong in itself in trying to improve a play of a predecessor. Shakespeare himself was the greatest of such improvers, and such transmutation as he accomplished excites our wonder, admiration, and gratitude. But in attempting such revision, if equal genius or talent to that of the creator is not required, at least good judgment, good taste, restraint, and a thorough knowledge of the principles of dramatic art, with the ability to apply them, are demanded. The trouble with most of the revisers was, as I have shown, that they did not understand Shakespeare's art, that they were led astray by false principles, and that they had no reverence for the great Elizabethan. Working in this spirit, their alterations and adaptations were almost always wretched failures, which in the long run have not injured Shakespeare, but have gained for their authors well-merited and everlasting contempt.

The foregoing account of the eighteenth-century (as for convenience we may designate the period under review) attitude towards and treatment of Shakespeare will have in a measure prepared, it is hoped, the way for the account of the alterations and adaptations in detail. In giving this, I shall confine myself practically to such altered versions or stage adaptations as exhibit marked or at least noticeable changes, mere acting versions of the plays not coming within the scope of the inquiry, and to those made previous to 1800. I shall usually make only incidental mention of any adaptations made after the beginning of the nineteenth century. By that time serious attempts to improve Shakespeare had virtually ceased, or, at least, nothing that would make a further contribution to our knowledge of the subject was produced. The playwright Frederick Reynolds, for instance, about 1820 turned several of Shakespeare's comedies into operas, which were wretchedly done and most of which he did not venture to print. No new principles or practices, however, were involved in these or any others.

My list of alterations and adaptations, which is based upon that given in the Old Variorum edition of Shakespeare, and which not only supplements but revises the catalogue there given, aims to be, and I may venture to hope that it is, as exhaustive an enumeration of these works as it is possible to make from the information and material which is obtainable or accessible. It is reasonable to believe that at least no important version has been omitted. In treating the plays I have adopted the order of the Globe edition.

II

THE ALTERATIONS AND ADAPTATIONS OF THE SEVERAL PLAYS

CHAPTER II. THE TEMPEST — THE TWO GENTLEMEN OF VERONA — THE MERRY WIVES OF WINDSOR

The Tempest

THE TEMPEST, a comedy so finished and delightful that it seems to our minds almost insusceptible of improvement, has been one of the chief sufferers at the hands of those who should have known better than to meddle with it.

The first attempt to improve it was made by D'Avenant and Dryden, and, to the eternal disgrace of these worthies, their revision is not only the worst one done by them but the worst produced by anybody and probably well-nigh the worst conceivable. Says Furness: "Unless we read it, no imagination, derived from a mere description, can adequately depict its monstrosity — to be fully hated it must be fully seen. Than this version, there is, I think, in the realm of literature no more flagrant instance to be found of *lèse-majesté*." Yet it was enthusiastically received, the house being, according to Pepys, who has six references to this play, "mighty full" at its representations.

It was written, as Pepys and the epilogue testify, in 1667, but was not printed until 1670, after D'Avenant's death. It was, as has been said before, one of those plays which D'Avenant selected for production as a dramatic opera, and accordingly it was furnished with elaborate scenery, music, and dancing.

But not content with additions of this sort, D'Avenant, who had some ideas about changes in the plot which seemed to him and to his friend Dryden most happy, set to work, with the help of his successor in the laureateship, to remodel the play in accordance with his theories. Dryden, in his preface to the first edition of the new play, expressly attributes to D'Avenant " the counterpart to Shakespeare's plot, namely, that of a man who had never seen a woman; that by this means the two characters of innocence and love might the more illustrate and commend each other." " This excellent contrivance," he goes on to say, " he was pleased to communicate to me, and to desire my assistance in it. I confess that from the very first moment it so pleased me, that I never writ anything with more delight." " The comical parts of the sailors " were also the invention of D'Avenant and were for the most part written by him, " as," Dryden says, " you will easily discover by the style."

The play was given the subtitle, " The Enchanted Island," and the following are the principal changes in the dramatis personæ. Alonso is Duke of Savoy and usurper of the Dukedom of Mantua, instead of King of Naples; Sebastian is omitted; Gonzalo, of course, is a nobleman of Savoy; Stephano is master of the ship, instead of a drunken butler; and Trincalo [*sic*] is boatswain. New characters are Hippolito, who had never seen a woman, heir of the Dukedom of Mantua; Mustacho, mate to Stephano; Ventoso, a mariner; Dorinda, sister to Miranda; Sycorax, sister to Caliban; and even Ariel has a duplicate in Milcha, to whom is given the song, " Full fathom five," etc. There were very elaborate scenic representations of a tempest and an enchanted island. Sometimes the diction is that of Shakespeare, but more often it departs widely from him, and there is much added, some of it indifferent but most of it very bad.

The First Act does not differ materially as to plot from the same act of the original until near the end, when Dorinda comes on and Miranda and she utter some of the most wretched stuff, about their chance of seeing a man, what he is like, and how he originates. The shipwreck scene is much altered as to language and for the worse, some of the new or modified orders being meaningless and others calculated to effect just the opposite of what was proper in the circumstances. Ariel's songs to Ferdinand are put in III, 1, and the remainder of the scene (2) is made the fourth scene of Act III.

The Second Act is considerably changed. The first scene is between Trincalo, Stephano, Mustacho, Ventoso, and Caliban, and is somewhat like Shakespeare's II, 2, but has much additional matter. Caliban's soliloquy is put into prose. In scene 2, Hippolito is introduced. He is warned by Prospero against woman, a creature he has never seen. Hippolito has just gone out when Miranda and Dorinda appear, to be in turn warned of the great danger that lies in man. After Prospero withdraws, the two sisters, in spite of their father's warning, make an attempt to see this dangerous creature. In the third scene, Hippolito enters, they see him, and Dorinda has a conversation with him. Scene 4 starts like II, 2, of the original, but soon changes greatly. The stage opens and a masque is given. Three devils sing under the stage, and Pride, Fraud, Rapine, and Murder sing solos and a chorus. This is intended to show Alonso, Antonio, and Gonzalo what crimes they have committed and to punish them.

The first scene of Act III consists of the two songs

of Ariel from Act I and the speeches of Ferdinand, the second song, as has been said, being sung by Ariel's duplicate Milcha. In scene 2, Prospero chides Miranda for disobeying him and not taking care of her sister; scolds Dorinda for her disobedience; and then commends Ariel for what he has done, commanding him to provide the prisoners with food and cheerful music. Ariel carries out his master's orders in scene 3. There is a dance of fantastic spirits and after that a table furnished with meat and fruit is brought in by two spirits. But on the prisoners' attempting to eat, the spirits fly away with the table. Then Caliban leads Trincalo to Sycorax and there is a ridiculous wooing of her by Trincalo. Trincalo gives her what he supposes is wine but water has been substituted for it by Ariel. Then enter Stephano, Mustacho, and Ventoso, who dispute with Trincalo about the sovereignty of the island. Scene 4 represents Ferdinand following Ariel. Ferdinand soliloquizes and sings to raise his spirits and Ariel echoes his soliloquy and song. This feature pleased the immortal diarist "mightily." Scene 5 is partly the omitted part of Act I, scene 2, and partly new matter, Prospero and Hippolito being the participants. Prospero refrains from chiding Hippolito because he sees that it is useless to try to bridle nature. Scene 6 is entirely new and is between Ferdinand and Hippolito, the latter proposing, in his innocence, to love both women, the former trying to persuade him that this is impossible.

Act IV opens with Prospero's giving Miranda leave to see Ferdinand and asking her to make him kindly disposed toward Hippolito. Miranda and Ferdinand talk and he becomes jealous of Hippolito. Soon afterwards, Hippolito and Dorinda talk together, Hippolito telling her that he loves her sister too and hurrying her away on the approach of Ferdinand. Ferdinand and Hippolito converse again, Ferdinand once more trying to show him that he must love only one, and at last they come to blows. Scene 2 is a drinking scene between the comic characters, ending in a quarrel, Sycorax driving off Caliban, and Trincalo, Stephano. Scene 3 is a long one. Ferdinand and Hippolito fight and the latter is wounded. Prospero blames Ariel for not preventing this; then enter Alonso, Gonzalo, and Antonio, and Prospero makes himself known to them. Dorinda is told by her father that all this misfortune has happened through breaking his precept and she scolds Miranda for letting her see a man. The act ends with a soliloquy by Ariel of about twenty rimed lines on the state of things on the island.

In the first scene of Act V, Miranda begs Prospero to pardon Ferdinand, which he refuses to do at first but afterwards does when Ariel comes in with news of Hippolito's restoration by the use of weapon salve, a medicament made by anointing the sword with various juices. Dorinda is by Hippolito's couch in the second scene, when Ferdinand and Miranda enter, and after a little playing at cross purposes all is made right. The former prisoners and the comic characters come in and the play ends much as in the original. The third scene is an elaborate masque provided by Prospero for the entertainment of the other characters, and consists of much dancing and singing by Neptune, Amphitrite, Oceanus, Tethys, and others. Ariel sings "Where the bee sucks," etc., and then a farewell between Prospero and him ends the play.

The outrageousness of this atrocious travesty is

so obvious even from a description of it that comment seems superfluous. Several features, however, may perhaps admit of a word of that nature. Making operatic additions to "The Tempest" is not an altogether bad treatment of it, for the play is of such a kind as to lend itself readily to the production of scenic effects and the introduction of music. If D'Avenant and Dryden had been content with this and had let the plot alone, one would not be disposed to blame them greatly, but the spoiling of such a beautiful play by making such a ridiculous thing of it is a black literary crime. The duplication and contrasting of characters is the most noticeable change. Shakespeare often repeats himself and contrasts characters, but always so as to contribute to the main purpose, one character or scene being kept subordinate that it may heighten the interest of another character or scene. Nowhere has he introduced such obvious counterparts as are characteristic of D'Avenant's "Macbeth" and the play under review. Scott has so well criticised this device that one cannot do better than to quote him. "Much cannot be said for D'Avenant's ingenuity in contrasting the character of a woman who had never seen a man, with that of a man who had never seen a woman, or in inventing a sister monster for Caliban. The majestic simplicity of Shakespeare's plan is injured by thus doubling his characters; and his wild landscape is converted into a formal parterre where 'each alley has its brother.' In sketching characters drawn from fancy and not from observation, the palm of genius must rest with the first inventor; others are but copyists, and a copy shows nowhere to such disadvantage as when placed by the original. Besides, although we are delighted with the feminine simplicity of Miranda, it becomes unmanly childishness in Hippolito; and the premature coquetry of Dorinda is disgusting when contrasted with the maidenly purity that chastens the simplicity of Shakespeare's heroine. The latter seems to display, as it were by instinct, the innate dignity of her sex; the former to show, even in solitude, the germ of those vices by which in a voluptuous age the female character becomes degraded." This great change gives rise to some of the most absurd situations and furnishes occasion for some of the silliest and otherwise most wretched dialogue to be found anywhere. Scott says further, "Miranda's simplicity is converted into indelicacy and Dorinda talks the language of prostitution before she has ever seen a man." The playing at cross purposes on the part of the two heroes and two heroines, while one of the legitimate conventions of the drama, is here so insipid and so prolix that it becomes exceedingly tiresome. Not satisfied with displaying lack of art by giving Caliban a sister, the authors must degrade him and the comic characters into low buffoons, who spend their time in nothing but quarreling, drinking, and foul talking. But this is only in keeping with the lowering of the tone of the whole play, done to please the taste and to conform to the morals of the time.

The device used to make Alonso, Antonio, and Gonzalo repent of their crimes is not nearly so imaginative as Shakespeare's. But the masque furnished opportunity for that singing, dancing, and scenic decoration which was the principal purpose of the alteration. The masque at the end, of course, is a legitimate introduction. It comes after the play proper has ended, and is really an afterpiece. Our authors doubtless omitted Shakespeare's masque of

Iris, Ceres, etc., because they thought their own to be better.

Saintsbury attributes the greater part of this travesty to D'Avenant, adducing, among other considerations, the verse which is "the strange disjointed blank verse, half prose, which was common between 1640 and 1660 and of which D'Avenant has left numerous examples, but which Dryden, almost from the first shook off."

In 1673, Dryden's literary enemy and successor in the laureateship, the dramatist Shadwell, made "The Tempest" into a regular opera, providing it with new scenes and elaborate stage machinery. It was produced at the theatre in Dorset Garden. Downes says that everything was admirably managed and no succeeding opera brought more money. We shall have to be content with this favorable opinion of its representation and this testimony as to its popularity, for Shadwell had sufficient sense not to print it, and so far as I know no description of it has survived.

D'Avenant's "Tempest" was, like his "Macbeth," ridiculed by Duffet, in this case, in a five-act farce, called "The Mock Tempest, or the Enchanted Castle," which was given at the Theatre Royal and which, according to Genest, "has some fun but not much." Another operatic travesty of this play was brought out at Edinburgh about the time of Garrick's opera (soon to be taken up). It was concocted out of Dryden and D'Avenant and some additional matter. Only the songs have been preserved. In 1780, there was printed at London, a three-act piece entitled "The Shipwreck, altered from Shakespeare and Dryden, with the original music by Smith, as performed at the Patagonian Theatre, Exeter Change." This was an absurd production, the witches in "Macbeth" being borrowed and spoiled. The only obligation to Dryden was the retention of Sycorax.

We have next to notice "The Tempest," an opera taken from Shakespeare," acted at Drury Lane in 1756 and printed the same year. The songs are said to be from Shakespeare, Dryden, etc., and an argument is prefixed. As in Dryden, Stephano is master of the ship, Trincalo is boatswain, the new characters Ventoso and Mustacho are introduced, and Sebastian is omitted. The author, who is probably Garrick, says by way of apology, "It is hoped that the reader will excuse the omission of many passages of the first merit, as they stand in the said play, it being impossible to introduce them in the plan of this opera." The echo episode is borrowed from Dryden and D'Avenant and enlarged, and in several passages the author follows their version rather than the original. Songs are inserted from Dryden and D'Avenant's "Tempest," from Dryden's "Tyrannic Love," and even from Ben Jonson (the last stanza of his beautiful lyric "Her Triumph" in "A Celebration of Charis"). This last is presumptive evidence of Garrick's authorship of this piece, as he was better read in old plays and other literature than most or all of his contemporaries. Prospero is made to sing, whereat Genest remarks, "If Garrick really made Prospero sing, he was quite right not to acknowledge it publicly, as, if he had avowed himself the compiler of this piece, every real friend to Shakespeare must have received his professions of respect for that author with a smile of contempt." He says further, "This opera is vastly superior to the generality of operas, but the attempt to reduce one of Shakespeare's plays to that despicable species of composition is in itself dramatic felony without benefit of clergy." It also speaks little for the sincerity of Garrick's regard for Shakespeare that, after he became manager, he revived the D'Avenant and Dryden "Tempest," although the original had been revived in 1746. Commercial reasons may have been largely responsible for this, however. Theophilus Cibber, in a dissertation which he delivered at the Haymarket in 1756, says of Garrick, referring to this opera and similar adaptations made by him: "Were Shakespeare's ghost to rise, would he not frown indignation on this pilfering pedler in poetry, who thus shamefully mangles, mutilates, and emasculates his plays? The 'Midsummer Night's Dream' has been minced and fricasseed into a thing called 'The Fairies,' 'The Winter's Tale' mammocked into a droll, and 'The Tempest' castrated into an opera. . . . Yet this sly prince would insinuate all this ill usage of the bard is owing, forsooth, to his love of him, much such a mock proof of his tender regard, as the cobbler's drubbing his wife. . . . No wonder Shakespeare's name is insulted by foreigners, while he is tamely suffered to be thus maltreated at home." This spirited castigation, while doubtless to a considerable extent called for, goes too far, and comes with bad grace from its author, who, we fear, was moved more by professional jealousy than by reverence for Shakespeare, against whom he had himself been an offender in a similar way.

In J. P. Kemble's revision of "The Tempest," which was acted at Drury Lane about fifteen times in 1789, the baneful influence of the D'Avenant-Dryden travesty is still potent, for Hippolito and Dorinda are retained, although Sycorax is rejected. The masque of Neptune and Amphitrite is also retained and the play is full of songs. The ridiculous shipwreck scene of D'Avenant and Dryden is replaced by Shakespeare's, but the restored scene is wrongly put in Act II. Kemble has restored a good deal of Shakespeare, particularly in the comic scenes, but often prefers D'Avenant and Dryden. He adds some of his own invention and sometimes alters what he takes from D'Avenant and Dryden. On the whole his alteration is a discredit to him and he must be numbered among those who have disgraced themselves by mutilating Shakespeare. When he revised his version for publication in 1815, he restored more of the original but still left the play sadly mangled.

The Two Gentlemen of Verona

This play was given in a somewhat altered form at Drury Lane, December 22, 1762. The reviser in this case was Benjamin Victor, a theatre manager for many years and the author of a history of the stage. Greatly to Victor's credit, he made no great changes in the plot, but was content with minor internal variations, some of which are judicious while others are unnecessary and in some cases absurd. He added a scene or two in order to make the comic element more prominent. None of the special principles of the Shakespeare revisers is involved in this version; but it may be of interest to notice briefly the alterations Victor made.

In the First Act, he has absurdly transposed scenes 2 and 3, thus making Julia answer Proteus's letter before she had received it, and further he has inserted here the 7th scene of Act II — Julia's consulting Lucetta about a journey to Milan, which in the original is only an afterthought of hers. Another ridiculous transposition has been made in the Second Act, by which our author brings it about that Silvia had not only determined to marry Valentine before he had plainly declared his love for her, but had even written a paper with directions for their marriage and escape. Launce speaks his first soliloquy at Milan instead of Verona. Acts III and IV differ little from the original. The short scene between Silvia and Eglamour has been judiciously transferred to Act IV. In the Fifth Act, Victor has made a great improvement by leaving out Valentine's overgenerous and foolish offer, "All that was mine in Silvia, I give thee." When Proteus offers to force Silvia, Valentine comes forward and orders the outlaws to seize him; he then speaks to Silvia, telling her to dismiss her fears as she is in safety; after which he reproaches Proteus and is reconciled to him. Victor has added two short scenes for the sake of bringing Launce and Speed on the stage in this act, but as the scenes are unnecessary and unworthy of Shakespeare, they had been better omitted.

J. P. Kemble revised Victor's alteration for representation at Covent Garden. In treating Acts I and II, he saw Victor's blunder in the case of the letter and corrected it, but he adopted some of Victor's changes for the worse, even his ridiculous consolidation of scenes 1 and 4 of Act II. For the rest, Kemble, although making no changes of plot, makes many unnecessary and wanton changes of words, gives names to the outlaws, and adds some of his own composition where there is no call for it. He follows Victor in discarding Valentine's unwarranted attempt to sacrifice himself on the altar of friendship.

These two treatments are chiefly interesting as showing how much care and dramatic taste and skill must be exercised in attempting to improve Shakespeare even in minor points, and how easy it is to fall into absurdities unless an improver has a complete grasp of the action of the play and the purpose of each detail.

The Merry Wives of Windsor

John Dennis, the critic, when replying to Rymer's absurd strictures, expressed a good deal of admiration for Shakespeare, although he held the opinion that he worked without art. Thinking further that he could improve some of Shakespeare's plays, he set to work to remodel "The Merry Wives of Windsor" in accordance with some of his dramatic notions. He also altered Coriolanus.

It seems strange that Dennis should have chosen the one comedy of Shakespeare's that Dryden, in his "Grounds of Criticism in Tragedy," had mentioned as regular in respect to the unities; but, as Dennis has given his reasons in his dedication of his revision to Granville, Lord Lansdowne, a recent predecessor in this line of endeavor, we will let him speak for himself. After saying that he chose this comedy because it is full of action, because it pleased Queen Elizabeth and Charles II and his court, and because he believed it to be susceptible of improvement, he goes on to say, with not a little vanity: "The Merry Wives of Windsor, as it has great beauties, so it has strange defects, which though they passed at first for the sake of the beauties, yet will come to be less endured as the stage grows more regular. For there are no less than three actions in it that are independent one of another, which divide and distract the minds of an audience; there is more than one insignificant scene, which has nothing to do with any other part of the play, which is enough to obstruct and stifle the action. The style in some places is stiff and forced and affected, whereas the dialogue in comedy ought to be as free as the air. This affectation is particularly remarkable in some parts of the first scene between the Wives, and in all Ford's part of the first scene between him and Falstaff. This is not said in the least with a design to derogate from Shakespeare's merit, who performed more than anyone else could have done in so short a time. In the alteration I have endeavored to correct the foresaid errors. I have made everything instrumental to Fenton's marriage, and the whole to depend on one common center, which I believe was hardly in the power of every writer to perform. I have added to some of the parts in order to heighten the characters and make them show the better. In short, I have altered everything which I disliked and retained everything which I or my friends approved of, excepting something of Justice Shallow in the first scene of the play, which I omitted for two reasons: the one was because I could not bring it into the same design with the rest, the second because I knew nobody who would be capable of acting that clear, unless those who would be otherwise employed. . . . Whether, sir, I have improved it or no, I leave it to you to determine: whether the scene between the Wives in the First Act be altered for the better or the worse; whether that between Falstaff and Ford in the Second Act is aptly contrived to give occasion to an excellent actor to show himself; whether that between Falstaff and the Wives in the Third Act be wholly without art, and whether that between Falstaff and Ford in the Fourth Act may be said to be truly comical." It may be said, in passing, that, judging from His Lordship's own production in this field, there can be no doubt that his decision was most favorable to the dedicator.

"The Comical Gallant, or the Amours of Sir John Falstaff" was the title Dennis gave to his play, which was brought out in 1702. He made few changes in the dramatis personæ. Mrs. Dorothy Tearsheet is substituted for Mrs. Quickly; Fenton is represented as nephew to Mrs. Ford, and his character and that of Anne Page are enlarged; Doctor Caius and Sir Hugh Evans are made less important; and a new character, the Host of the Bull, brother to Mrs. Ford, is added. The change of Brook to Broom was not original with Dennis, but had crept into the prompt-books before the Folio of 1623.

The conduct of the action is much altered to adapt it to the notions put forth in the dedication. Act I opens with a scene between Fenton and the Host of the Garter, the latter of whom is asked by Fenton to get Sir Hugh, who is promoting Slender's suit to Anne Page, into trouble with Doctor Caius. Anne Page comes in, in response to a letter previously carried to her by the Host. Fenton tells her what he has asked that worthy to do, also that he has persuaded Falstaff that Mrs. Page and Mrs. Ford are in love with him, and that he has also persuaded two of Falstaff's men to betray him to Ford and Page. Then enter Falstaff, Shallow, Slender, and others, and the scene is like I, 1 of the original. Falstaff discharges Pistol and Nym as in I, 3 (lines from I, 2 being added). The Host carries out his part with regard to Caius and Evans. The Wives compare their letters, and the act concludes with a scene in which Pistol and Nym inform Ford and Page of Falstaff's intentions. A great deal of Shakespeare's dialogue is used in this act, but there is much that is new.

Act II opens with Shakespeare's II, 3. Then Ford, disguised as Broom, hires Falstaff to seduce his wife. Hardly any of the language here is Shakespeare's except the soliloquy at the end, and Dennis's dialogue is extremely coarse. The remainder of the act is almost exactly like III, 1 of the original.

The first scene of Act III is like Shakespeare's III, 3, except that the scene is at the Bull Inn and that the new character, the Host of the Bull, is introduced. Mrs. Page is at first absent, but she enters, while Falstaff and Mrs. Ford are talking, disguised as Captain Dingboy, a gallant who pretends to be on a similar errand to Falstaff's. Falstaff takes refuge behind the arras, but discloses himself when Mrs. Page vilifies him. They call each other names and she frightens Falstaff with a pistol, Falstaff roaring with fear. On Ford's approach, the "fat knight" is carried off in the buck-basket. Mrs. Page then gives Ford a beating, but Mrs. Ford and she run out when the latter's wig is pulled off.

In Act IV, Ford again interviews Falstaff at the Bull. After Falstaff goes out, the Host tells Ford that his wife and Falstaff are to meet at Herne's Oak at midnight. To circumvent this the Host and Ford devise a plan, the principal features of which are that Ford is to go to the rendezvous dressed like Falstaff and that the Host is to tell Mrs. Ford that her husband has gone to London. The next scene is between Fenton and Anne Page, and in it he tells her to dress not as her father or her mother desires, but in a suit he will leave for her at Mrs. Ford's. The last scene is between Anne, Shallow, and Slender, and some of it is like the last part of I, 1 of the original.

Act V consists of the dénouement at Herne's Oak. Falstaff, after entering to Mrs. Ford and Mrs. Page, secretes himself on hearing a "terrible symphony." All the pinching and beating by the supposed fairies goes to Ford, disguised as Falstaff, while the latter not only escapes unhurt but comes in to see the sport. The remainder is much as in Shakespeare save that the Host of the Garter, disguised as a parson, marries Doctor Caius to Slender, and that Fenton and Anne come in unmarried and obtain forgiveness before the ceremony of their marriage is performed. The play ends with a moral directed against clandestine marriages. Such is the miserable production upon which our ingenuous author felicitated himself, believing he had made an improvement on Shakespeare. Dullness, like Love, is evidently blind — rendered purblind or stone-blind in this instance by inordinate vanity.

Let us see how Dennis's would-be improvements compare with their originals and stand the test of dramatic art and common sense. One great change is the omission of Falstaff's second visit to Mrs. Ford, made, as we have seen, to do away with one of the so-called independent actions. Dennis was not able to make it fit in with his plan of making everything instrumental to Fenton's marriage. One may be pardoned for asking why, with this end in view, he did not also admit Falstaff's first visit, which, so far as we can see, contributes very little or not at all to that end, and why, deeming the marriage the most important thing in the play, he did not give his remodeled play a title indicative of his view. In reality, in spite of all this, Falstaff's adventures are made the main interest, and we are sorry to be deprived of a third part of them, especially when, for aught anyone can see, the omitted episode is just as conducive as the retained one to the professed end. How much more natural and artistic are Shakespeare's method of setting Sir Hugh and Doctor Caius at variance and his making Falstaff of himself become amorous of the Wives, than Dennis's artificial expedient of making Fenton the bringer about of both conditions!

Dennis's common-center theory led him to try to make what in Shakespeare's play is the secondary plot the main action, but he makes wretched work of his attempt. How could he fail to see the masterly dramatic skill of the Elizabethan in combining so consummately two actions, the amorous intrigues of Falstaff and the love affairs of Anne Page. How clearly does he exhibit that lack of art which he attributed to his predecessor!

Another marked change is the action in the Third Act. The necessity for the change of the place of Falstaff's interview with the Wives and for the addition of the Host of the Bull is not evident. It is much more natural that Falstaff should go to Ford's house. Mrs. Page's masquerading as an eighteenth-century spark, while doubtless pleasing to the audiences of Dennis's time, makes the character a dreadful caricature of the right-minded wife of the original. Our reviser's conduct of the action in the entire act is most unskilful as compared with that of Shakespeare. We are disgusted with the representation of Falstaff as roaring like a frightened bull before a pistol in the hand of the disguised Mrs. Page, and of Ford as receiving a beating from her.

Mention of this last episode suggests and will serve to introduce the greatest dramatic change in the play, the depression of the character of Ford. In Shakespeare's play the jealous but dignified husband, when events and appearances are explained to him, begs his wife's pardon and joins with the Wives in the attempt to punish Falstaff at Herne's Oak. But Dennis has changed all that. The motive of the meeting at the oak becomes, instead of an endeavor to punish Falstaff for his lust, an attempt to cure Ford of his jealousy. Even this purpose is clumsily executed. Dennis, in making this dénouement, brought his play into conformity with that immorality which characterized the Restoration comedies, in which the injured husband is made to suffer ridicule, while the profligate gallant who has tampered with the wife gets off scot free with commendation and applause.

Minor changes of action may be dismissed with the simple statement that they are uniformly bad and often absurd.

With regard to the dialogue, while Dennis frequently follows Shakespeare closely, more than half of it is new. His attempt to make the dialogue "free" has certainly succeeded in one sense, for he has made it far coarser. There will be no dissent from the conclusion that this is an execrable alteration.

CHAPTER III. MEASURE FOR MEASURE—THE COMEDY OF ERRORS—MUCH ADO ABOUT NOTHING—LOVE'S LABOUR'S LOST

Measure for Measure

D'AVENANT'S "Law against Lovers" is an alteration of "Measure for Measure," with the incorporation of the characters of Benedick and Beatrice from "Much Ado about Nothing." This seems to be the first of these *rifacimenti*, for it was produced as early as February, 1662, at the theatre in Lincoln's Inn Fields, although it was not printed until 1673.

The characters of "Measure for Measure" are mostly retained, as are also the chief features of the main plot, but the comic underplot is omitted. The borrowed characters are fitted into the dramatis personæ by making Benedick a brother of Angelo and Beatrice a cousin of Julietta and ward of Angelo. A new character is added in Viola, who is a very young sister to Beatrice, and who, Benedick says, "is not a chip of the old block, but will prove a smart twig of the young branch," and whose singing and dancing especially pleased Pepys. Very little of the action of "Much Ado" is introduced, but many extracts from its dialogue are made use of, being joined in a somewhat altered form with dialogue of D'Avenant's own manufacture. The scene is shifted to Turin.

At the opening of Act I, the Duke entrusts the government to Angelo and Escalus as in Shakespeare.

Then enter Beatrice, Julietta, Viola, and Balthasar (who has also been imported, somewhat altered, from " Much Ado "), and the scene is like I, 1 of " Much Ado." On the announcement of Benedick's entrance, the ladies step behind the hangings and then Escalus informs Benedick that the latter's brother is now the head of the government. Lucio comes in and tells of the revival of an old law, which is considered a law against lovers (whence the new title). Beatrice, Julietta, and Viola then appear and the wit combat between Benedick and Beatrice from " Much Ado about Nothing " I, 1, follows. Viola is a sort of duplication of Beatrice. All of the company next go to the presence of Angelo, who is expecting them, except Lucio, to whom a servant makes known Claudio's imprisonment. The rest of the act is made up of " Measure for Measure " I, 3, 4, and 5, the altered Balthasar being unnecessarily introduced as one of the characters in the action.

Act II is at first like " Measure for Measure " II, 1 down to " Enter Elbow, etc.," except that Benedick has the part of Escalus. Angelo then goes out and Escalus enters and informs Benedick that Angelo wants to marry his brother (Benedick) to his ward (Beatrice). Thereupon Benedick and Lucio and Balthasar, who enter a little later utter some of the words of Benedick against marriage from " Much Ado about Nothing " I, 1. Then appear Beatrice and Viola and there follows a wit combat between Benedick and Beatrice in imitation of Shakespeare. Scenes 2 and 3 of " Measure for Measure " II, are introduced next. The scene shifts to the prison, where Lucio and Balthasar comfort Claudio, who entrusts Julietta to their protection. The act ends with a part of " Measure for Measure " II, 4.

Act III opens with the rest of II, 4. Benedick and Beatrice then have a scene, professedly in imitation of Shakespeare. She asks him to steal his brother's seal and use it to free Claudio. Viola enters and sings a song she says has been composed by Lucio. After the song, Lucio and Balthasar come on the scene and Lucio avers that Benedick composed the song and is in love with Beatrice. Beatrice says she loves another, "suppose it is Signor Lucio." This causes Lucio to change face and say that Benedick is not in love with her, his assertion to that effect having been made, he says, to get an opportunity to sue for himself. That part of "Measure for Measure," III, 1, in which the characters who take part are Isabella, Claudio, and the Duke, is then introduced, with some changes. In the next scene, Benedick tells Beatrice that he has obtained the seal and, after she goes out, Escalus, who has stolen the seal, asks Benedick to secure him in case the plot fails. A short scene in which Viola is visiting Julietta in prison (in Shakespeare she is not put in prison, and takes little part in the action) ends the act.

Act IV is almost all D'Avenant's. Among others, there is a scene in which Benedick tells Beatrice that they are likely to be circumvented by a friar and in which, on her advising that everything be made to appear right to the deputy, they make merry and have some dancing, a saraband being danced by Viola; and a scene in which Isabella visits the imprisoned Julietta, who implores her to yield to Angelo, but who, on Isabella's proposing that she take her place in such a proceeding, is brought to herself. The rest of the act is made up of some stuff between Benedick and Beatrice, in the course of which it is made evident that their plot is discovered; of the execution of Bernardine, somewhat like IV, 3; of the formation of a plot by Claudio for Julietta's escape; and, finally, of a scene between Angelo and Isabella, in which he, after vainly trying to induce her to yield to him, declares he is only testing her virtue.

The dénouement in Act V is so peculiar that a somewhat detailed description of it may perhaps be pardoned. At the beginning, Viola, Lucio, Beatrice, and Benedick sing verses of a song and chorus in the hearing of Angelo to hide an attempt by a party, headed by Benedick, to rescue Claudio, which attempt is defeated by the Duke (as a friar). Benedick has been partly successful, but the Provost exhibits a head supposed to be Claudio's from the battlements. The Duke then makes himself known and orders Angelo and Benedick to be put in prison. After much roundabout action, Angelo, who supposes himself lost when Claudio is reported dead, comes out in safety and is given Isabella; Claudio, who, of course, has not been killed, is made happy with Julietta; and Benedick and Beatrice are brought together. As will have been noticed, the character of Mariana has been rejected altogether. Such is the wretched hodgepodge which D'Avenant had the effrontery to put forward as an improvement on Shakespeare.

The chief dramatic change is seen to be in the conception of Angelo, who, instead of being a scoundrel who meets with a better fate than he deserves, is made, as the hero of the play, a model of virtue, whose attempt to seduce Isabella is represented as simply a curious experiment to find a wife for the good man who is to be the Duke's (an old man in D'Avenant) successor. The reason for this elevation of Angelo was to have a thoroughly estimable hero, who should conform to that "rule of art," which requires the hero and heroine to be without actual blemish. Decidedly is this treatment inferior to Shakespeare's, the action being more clumsily managed and the omission of Mariana depriving us of the pathos of Angelo's treachery to her.

In this play is the first manifestation of a dramatic theory and practice which characterizes D'Avenant's alterations. I refer to that duplication of characters and scenes which appears in only too full development in his "Macbeth" and in his and Dryden's "Tempest." Here it is little more than a slight anticipation, the character of Viola being introduced more to give occasion for singing and dancing than to "illustrate" or "commend" the character of Beatrice.

Of the reprehensible device of lifting Benedick and Beatrice from "Much Ado" and thrusting them in here, where they really are out of place and unnecessary, little need be said. The only conceivable reason for it was to provide spicy dialogue for the audience. D'Avenant knew that these characters in Shakespeare furnish abundance of it and he was fatuous enough to believe he could improve on it and imitate it.

D'Avenant, as usual with his kind, takes unwarrantable liberties with Shakespeare's diction, often changing it out of mere caprice. Much of what he adds of his own composition is put in rime. This all results in some of the most wretched poetry — it is almost straining courtesy to give it that name — to be found in the realm of the drama.

There is to be noticed, also, the significant change in moral attitude shown by the new title. In Shakespeare, the old law, the revival of which is responsible for Claudio's imprisonment, is not regarded as a law against lovers in general, but against illicit lovers.

Shakespeare's title is sufficiently indicative of his higher moral point of view.

In conclusion I cannot do better than to quote Charles Knight's comment on this play, and on the alterations generally, in his "History of Opinion on the Writings of Shakespeare:" "'The Law against Lovers' was in principle one of the worst of these alterations; for it was a hash of two plays. . . . This was indeed to destroy the organic life of the author. But it is one of the manifestations of the vitality of Shakespeare that, going about their alterations in the regular way, according to the rules of art, the most stupid and prosaic of his improvers have been unable to deprive the natural man of his vigor, even by their most violent depletions."

This play was again altered by the dramatist and critic, Charles Gildon, one of the half-hearted defenders of Shakespeare against Rymer and his kind. Gildon admired Shakespeare, but deprecated his "lack of art." So, to give an example of what Shakespeare might have done if he had had the knowledge of dramatic principles that our critic's living in a later and more enlightened age and his greater learning had brought to him, he attempted to improve "Measure for Measure." Unfortunately for Mr. Gildon, he only made evident thereby his own lack of genius and of genuine dramatic art. The full title of Gildon's remodeling is "Measure for Measure, or Beauty the Best Advocate, written originally by Mr. Shakespeare and now very much altered with additions of several entertainments of music." It was acted and printed in 1760. The prologue by Oldmixon, a part of which is quoted, is interesting for its depreciatory comment on the taste of the time.

> "No more let labored scenes, with pain, be wrought,
> What least is wanting in a play is thought.
> Let neither dance, nor music, be forgot,
> Nor scenes, no matter for the sense or plot.
> Such things we own in Shakespeare's days might do,
> But then his audience did not judge like you."

The scene is laid in Turin, as in D'Avenant, and the borrowed character of Balthasar is another change for which Gildon was indebted to his predecessor. The comic underplot is, of course, likewise rejected.

In Act I, Lucio tells Balthasar, who has just returned from the wars, that the Duke is to travel incognito, that Angelo has been made deputy, and that Claudio must die to-morrow on account of the revival of old laws, although Escalus has pleaded for him and has provided music and opera to melt Angelo. Then follows a scene like parts of Shakespeare's II, 1 and II, 2. It may be interesting to quote at this point a passage from the latter, as transformed by the two revisers, for the sake of comparing both with the original and Gildon's with D'Avenant's. Thereby will be exhibited the result of the "refining" of the barbarous language of Shakespeare and will be disclosed in full measure Gildon's obligation to D'Avenant, which he failed to acknowledge.

> "If men could thunder
> As great Jove does, we ne'er should be at quiet.
> For every cholerick petty officer
> Would use the magazine of heaven for thunder;
> Nothing but thunder: Oh! Merciful heaven!
> Thou rather with thy sharp and sulphurous bolt
> Dost split the knotty and obdurate oak
> Than the soft myrtle. Oh! but man, proud man

> (Dressed in a little brief authority,
> Most ignorant of what he thinks himself
> Assured), in his frail glassy essence, like
> An angry ape, plays such fantastic tricks
> Before high heaven, as would make angels laugh,
> If they were mortal and had spleens like us."

So Gildon; now let us have D'Avenant.

> If men could thunder
> As great Jove does, Jove ne'er would quiet be.
> For every cholerick petty officer
> Would use his magazine in heaven for thunder;
> We nothing should but thunder hear. Sweet heaven!
> Thou rather with thy stiff and sulphurous bolt
> Dost split the knotty and obdurate oak
> Than the soft myrtle. O but man, proud man,
> Drest in a little brief authority,
> Most ignorant of what he thinks himself
> Assured, does in his glassy essence, like
> An angry ape, play such fantastic tricks
> Before high heaven, as would make angels laugh,
> If they were mortal and had spleens like us."

Isabella is told by Angelo to return " as soon as the opera is over," and then is given the first " entertainment " of " The Loves of Dido and Æneas, a mask in four musical entertainments." At the end of the act, Angelo soliloquizes on his love for Isabella.

Act II opens like II, 4. If Isabella is going to comply with Angelo's desire she is to meet him at the opera. In the second scene, Angelo tells the solicitous Escalus that he shall rigorously enforce the law in the case of Claudio, and then the second entertainment is given. Angelo declares that it is unavailing to ease his pain. In the third scene, which is at the prison, Friar Thomas informs the Duke that the latter has long been mistaken in Angelo, who, the Friar declares, is married to Mariana. The Duke in the next scene visits Claudio and becomes convinced of his innocence. A little is borrowed here from Shakespeare's I, 3 and II, 3. In the last scene of the act, the Duke interviews Julietta, who is also in prison, as in D'Avenant. She declares herself married to Claudio and the Duke promises to help them.

Act III, scene 1 is for the most part like Shakespeare's III, 1, but besides some alterations by Gildon has additions from D'Avenant. The conversation between the Duke and Isabella is put in verse. In scene 2, the third entertainment is given before Angelo and others. Angelo speaks of contradictory letters from the Duke and says, "No Isabella yet." She enters, however, at the close of the entertainment.

Act IV, scene 1, is a third scene between Angelo and Isabella, in which Gildon again borrows from D'Avenant. Angelo tries to persuade her to yield to him and gives her a casket of diamonds, which she takes, as she says aside, to give to Mariana as proof of Angelo's guilt. She promises to return in two hours. Scene 2 is like IV, 1 of the original. Isabella gives Mariana the casket and tells her to take her place with Angelo. Scene 3, which is at the prison, is like Shakespeare's IV, 2 from "Enter Claudio" to Angelo's letter to the provost, inclusive. Then Julietta and Claudio have a farewell interview, at the end of which she faints and is carried off. The provost is convinced of Claudio's innocence and tells the Duke (friar) he will do as he advises. Isabella enters and has an interview with the Duke as in IV, 3.

Act V is badly mangled. Scene 1 is partly like IV, 4 and partly like V, 1 (somewhat shortened). Angelo is immediately denounced by the Duke, who says that he was himself contriver of this scene and that Angelo shall be executed on the same block on which Claudio was. The play is then made to end about as in Shakespeare. As another example of the reviser's own lack of art may be instanced the fact that the lines of the Duke's, asking Angelo to forgive the provost for having sent him Ragozine's head for Claudio's, are retained although the part of the third scene of Act IV relating to the sending of the pirate's head has been omitted. At the conclusion all the characters listen to the fourth entertainment.

This alteration was avowedly made to make the play more palatable by the addition of spectacle, music, and dancing. Indeed, it almost seems as if the entertainments were more important than the play itself, which is manipulated to make occasion for them. However, they are out of place, are insipid, cause the omission of much of the original, and disfigure and cheapen the play. They were doubtless suggested, as are many things in the conduct of the action, by the "Law against Lovers." This play copies that one in the depression of characters, especially that of Isabella. It was highly contemptible in Gildon to borrow from that source, particularly without acknowledgment. The only commendation that can be given to Gildon is for retaining so much more than D'Avenant did of Shakespeare's play and for rejecting the additions from "Much Ado about Nothing." But when all allowances are made, Gildon's production is a sad mutilation, possessing interest only as another example of the results of that fondness for operatic features which disfigured so many of the representations of Shakespeare's plays during the eighteenth century.

ALTERATIONS AND ADAPTATIONS

The Comedy of Errors

This play, which was a romanticization of a classical farce and which observed the unities of time and place, virtually afforded no opportunity for alteration along the lines of academic principles of art, and so we find none. A number of adaptations of part or all of it were made, however, but they will call for little more than bare mention, and in two cases that is all that can be given.

The first is a farce called "Everybody Mistaken," which was given at Lincoln's Inn Fields in March, 1716, and, according to one authority, is by one William Taverner. It was never printed and its relation to its original is unknown.

The second is a comedy with the title "All Mistaken," by William Shirley. The Biographia Dramatica says it had great additions but was neither printed nor acted.

The adaptation by Hull, deputy manager of Covent Garden Theatre, given there in 1779, does not differ materially from the original. Says Mrs. Inchbald, in her remarks on this play: "This drama was scarcely known to the stage of the last century, till Mr. Hull . . . curtailed and made other judicious alterations and arrangements, by which it was rendered attractive for some nights, and afterwards placed upon the list of plays that are generally performed during every season." Later opinion may differ with her as to the wisdom of making such changes as that of "chain" to bracelet, and numerous others almost equally unnecessary and wanton; of adding much of his own versifying; of leaving out some of the best (as the description of Pinch); of introducing a new character, Hermia, a cousin to Adriana, simply to sing a song; and, lastly, of tagging on the ridiculous moral:

> " Our lesson this
> That misery past endears our present bliss,
> Wherein we read with wonder and delight,
> This sacred truth, ' Whatever is, is right.' "

The fourth is a three-act comedy entitled " The Twins, or Which is Which," composed by a Mr. William Woods, performed at Edinburgh in 1780, and printed in a collection of farces in 1786. Act I consists of Shakespeare's I, 2, II, 2, and III, 1, with abridgments, and various passages from the omitted scenes. Antipholus of Syracuse, for instance, is made to relate the early history of his family as given in the omitted first scene of Act I. Act II is made up of parts of III, 2, IV, 1, and IV, 4, while Act III is V, 1, much abridged. No change is made in the plot.

Much Ado about Nothing

D'Avenant's " Law against Lovers," in which some of the characters and much of the dialogue of " Much Ado about Nothing " are amalgamated with " Measure for Measure," is fully described under that play, and so need not detain us here.

One of the strangest of all the alterations of Shakespeare is that made of this play by the forgotten dramatist James Miller, under the title of " The Universal Passion," which was acted nine times and printed in 1737. The Old Variorum editors put it down as a pasticcio of " Much Ado about Nothing," " As You Like It," and " Love's Labour's Lost." This is far from being true, for there is nothing from either of the latter two. Another writer describes it as an alteration of "All's Well that Ends Well." It is evident that these authorities had not read or even glanced at Miller's play. Anyone seeing simply the list of characters might easily be led to think it an amalgamation of several of Shakespeare's plays, but there is no excuse for stating an unverified inference as a fact.

The play is, in truth, a wretched jumble of "Much Ado about Nothing" and Molière's "Princess of Elis." Miller in his prologue acknowledges his indebtedness to Shakespeare, but says nothing of Molière.

The scene is laid at Genoa, and the characters (with their Shakespearean equivalents) are as follows:

        Protheus, a nobleman of Genoa (Benedick);
        Joculo, the court jester;
        Bellario, a young Venetian lord (Claudio);
        Gratiano, the Duke of Genoa (Leonato);
        Byron, bastard brother to the Duke (Don John);
        Gremio (Borachio and Conrade);
        Lucentius;
        Porco (Dogberry);
        Asino (Verges);
        Lucilia (Hero);
        Liberia (Beatrice);
        Delia (Margaret).

Most of the First Act is from Molière, somewhat altered. Bellario is in love with Lucilia, but, as she is in the habit of treating her suitors with contempt, he determines to affect indifference to her. He engages Joculo to help him. Gratiano, the father of Lucilia, expresses to her his wish that she should marry, and she declares to him her aversion to matrimony. The remainder of the act, consisting mostly of a wit combat between Protheus and Liberia, is from the first and third scenes of the First Act of "Much Ado."

Molière furnishes almost all of Act II, although some dialogue is taken from Shakespeare. The action is chiefly occupied with the affairs of Bellario and Lucilia, each of whom pretends to be in love with someone else.

In the Third Act, the first part of which is chiefly from Molière, Lucilia consents to take Bellario after Joculo tells her that her suitor has rescued her father from two ruffians and after her father himself urges her to do so. At this point Miller deserts Molière. Lucilia is speedily and completely metamorphosed into Shakespeare's Hero, and the play follows "Much Ado" in the main, though with many changes in minor details, from Don Pedro's proposal, in Act II, 1, to bring about a match between Benedick and Beatrice, to the end.

In attempting to improve upon his original, the reviser has fallen into many absurdities. In particular, the Fifth Act is badly confused. For example, he introduces a scene between Joculo and Delia in which she begs that worthy to intercede for her with Lucilia, at a time when that lady is supposed to be dead.

Miller alters the dialogue greatly, introduces lines from "Twelfth Night" and "Two Gentlemen of Verona," and altogether has succeeded in making a most wretched amalgamation of two good plays.

It cannot be supposed that a compilation from Shakespeare and Molière should be a wholly bad play. Even the most violent treatment cannot rob two such geniuses of their vigor, but they have certainly suffered sadly at the hands of Miller. It is not worth while to do more than censure the general principle this alteration exhibits. To make a play by combining different plays of the same author's, or plays in the same language, is bad enough, but to make one out of the plays of authors writing in different languages is too contemptible a practice on which to waste any words. Besides, in this case, what an absurdity to metamorphose suddenly Molière's vivacious heroine, who somewhat resembles Beatrice, into the quiet-spirited Hero!

As a final word on Miller's lack of art, it may be said that whenever he varies from his originals he alters for the worse and often succeeds in spoiling scenes or characters. All will agree that this is about the most outrageous instance conceivable of want of reverence for two great masters. The length to which a would-be improver of Shakespeare may go is here strikingly exemplified.

Love's Labour's Lost

There exists a rather curious alteration of this play which was never acted but has been printed. The title page reads, "The Students, a comedy altered from Shakespeare's Love's Labour's Lost and adapted to the stage, 1762." Apparently its merit was not regarded even in those days as sufficient to achieve its avowed purpose. Its author, who has wisely chosen to remain unknown, has occasionally made perhaps a minor improvement, but for the most part his changes, especially in the characterizations and dialogue, are bad.

The play is furnished with a prologue and epilogue. In the former there is incidentally exhibited evidence of the fact that Shakespeare was popular with the masses, and that by this time they were getting disgusted with the mutilated versions, the so-called improvements, of his plays that were presented for their approval by those who deemed themselves the masters of dramatic art. The author says:

> " Should he fail, he hopes the wits will own,
> There's enough of Shakespeare's still, to please the town."

The characters of Holofernes and Sir Nathaniel are omitted.

Up to the third scene of Act II, the play is mostly like Shakespeare's first two acts, with the exception of considerable omission and rearrangement. It may be mentioned, in passing, that the rime is removed in the revision of the dialogue. At this point a new scene is introduced between Costard and Jaquenetta, which is very silly, as he is afraid to say much to her. The fourth scene has some new features. A clown comes in carrying a coat for Costard, which Biron takes and puts on to make himself look like its owner. After the departure of the clown, Biron soliloquizes as at the end of Shakespeare's Third Act.

Act III opens with the King's reading the poem of IV, 3, " So sweet a kiss," etc. Biron, dressed like Costard, takes up the paper. The King goes out, and then Dumain enters and asks the supposed Costard to take his paper to Katharine. After Dumain's exit, Longaville appears and gives the messenger a missive for Maria. The second scene opens with a few lines from IV, 1. Then Rosaline boasts that Biron is her slave, but Maria says the others are content with a more moderate love. Biron, as Costard, comes on the scene and gives papers to the Princess, Katharine, and Maria, who thereupon laugh at the

ALTERATIONS AND ADAPTATIONS

recently boastful Rosaline because there is none for her. Katharine reads "On a day, alack the day!" but the others do not read. They are afraid of being tricked, so they tell Biron to return the messages with the answer that they are not to be wooed. In the third scene, Biron meets Jaquenetta, who thinks study has improved Costard. The real Costard then comes in, but Biron succeeds in outfacing him and convincing Jaquenetta that he is the true Costard. After Biron and she go out, Dumain enters and gives Costard a beating on his denying having had any letter for Katharine. The poor fool by this time neither knows where he is nor who he is.

In the first scene of the next act, Armado tells Dull to apprehend Costard. In the second scene, Biron, as Costard, gives the King and Dumain the returned missives, but exchanges them and in this way the love affairs are discovered. Biron then goes out, but soon reappears in his own character and pokes fun at his companions, who are unable to make him confess being in love. Dull, Costard, Armado, and Jaquenetta enter, Armado accuses Costard of what Biron has done, and poor Costard is declared to be mad and ordered to be confined. After the principal characters leave the scene, Armado makes love to Jaquenetta and is discovered thus doing by Biron, who has returned to order him to prepare a masque to entertain the Princess and the other ladies. Some speeches from V, 2, are used in the third scene. Boyet announces that the king and the others are coming with "some scene of merriment or antic show." The ladies agree together not to listen to the wooing of the men.

In Act V, the first scene is between Armado and a player. Armado asks him to present the masque of the Nine Worthies, but he prefers to give a comic dance. The second scene includes much of Shakespeare's V, 2, and IV, 3. The suits of the men appear to be about to fail completely, when Biron tries his hand on Rosaline, who, at last, on his threatening to leave, gives up resistance with, "I was only joking," and then all is over. The "antic" scene is then given and the play ends. Love's labor is not lost, even temporarily. There is to be no waiting a twelvemonth, so Shakespeare's

> "Our wooing doth not end like an old play;
> Jack hath not Jill; these ladies' courtesy
> Might well have made our sport a comedy,"

becomes

> "Our wooing now doth end like an old play;
> Jack has his Jill; these ladies' courtesy
> Hath nobly made our sport a comedy."

Practically the only reason discoverable for making this alteration appears to be to produce a new play with numerous farcical situations. No principle of art seems to have been especially involved. The author apparently thought that the characters of Holofernes and Sir Nathaniel, in whom Shakespeare satirized mere phrase-making, detracted from the unity of the comedy, and so omitted them. This is doubtless a judicious change for stage purposes, as their pedantic phraseology, however amusing in the closet, could not have been very attractive to an audience. Perhaps the chief change in the action is the different way of making Biron acquainted with the fact that his comrades are forsworn. That, simply by putting on Costard's coat, he could be so completely disguised as not to be recognized by his friends, necessitates too great a draft on the imagination. The situation is not an easy one to manage anyhow, but Shakespeare's art, even when, as here, it is far short of its future development, has contrived much better than his unknown "improver." The character of Biron is degraded by making the part, to a considerable extent, that of a buffoon. Costard, who is introduced in the original simply to be an instrument to betray Biron to his friends, is made too prominent here, but this is for the sake of farce. Keeping the friends so long ignorant of each other's falling in love is an unnecessary change, it being better to have them find each other out and so to act in concert in furthering their suits than to make Biron betray them to each other as he does in this play. The ladies' disguising themselves and making each of the suitors pay court to the wrong mistress is much better comedy, as paying them back in their own coin, than their simply holding out to give in at last. One minor change seemed to Genest a "happy" one, namely, the omission of Armado's letter to the king as a letter and the putting of the contents into the character's lines. We strongly doubt if this adaptation would have been a marked success, even in its day, had it succeeded in being put on the stage.

CHAPTER IV. A MIDSUMMER NIGHT'S DREAM — THE MERCHANT OF VENICE — AS YOU LIKE IT — THE TAMING OF THE SHREW

A Midsummer Night's Dream

THE list of treatments of the whole or of parts of this play is one of the longest of its kind, but none of them are of much importance and there is consequently little to be said.

The first in the catalogue is "The Humours of Bottom the Weaver" by Robert Cox. This, a copy of which I have not seen, is, as its title and author indicate, a droll, as such plays were called, or farce, made up, in this instance, from the comic parts of Shakespeare's play. These drolls were performed, while the stage was suppressed, by stealth, under the pretence of rope dancing. The author of this one, Cox, used to act the principal parts himself, and he became a great favorite both in London and in the country.

"A Midsummer Night's Dream" was performed as an opera at the Theatre Royal in 1692 under the title of "The Fairy Queen." The author is unknown. On the whole, it does not differ materially, as to plot and action, from the original. Some changes are made in the dialogue, there is some omission and transposition, and a great deal of singing, dancing, and machinery is introduced. Downes says that the court and town were wonderfully satisfied with "The Fairy Queen," but that the expense was so great the company got very little by it. The lyric and spectacular elements of "A Midsummer Night's Dream" make turning it into an opera of this kind more legitimate than so treating almost any other Shakespearean play, and no great condemnation is merited for doing it. In this case, however, the author, as it but too usual in such adaptations, altered and omitted unwarrantably and sometimes absurdly.

Next on the list is "Pyramus and Thisbe," a comic masque, by Richard Leveridge, 1716. In this, the burlesque interlude of Shakespeare's play is put into the form of an Italian opera with the object of ridiculing that species of dramatic exhibition, which the English had taken up and become extravagantly fond of, to the detriment and neglect of more meritorious music and drama — so much so indeed, that Addison was constrained to write strongly against it. Let Leveridge speak for himself as to the character of his piece. "I have made bold," he says, "to dress out the original in recitative and airs after the present Italian mode." The dialogue differs but little from Shakespeare, but there are three new characters, Semibreve, the composer, and his friends Crotchet and Gamut. The latter two make the comments on the singing, etc., and Semibreve replies to them in a way satirical of the Italian opera. For instance, when the wall has sung, Gamut observes, "This is the most musical partition I ever heard." Semibreve answers, "This is nothing to what we have abroad and by degrees I am in hopes to bring our dull English to this polite taste." Crotchet wonders whether the lion is to sing. Semibreve answers, "Never wonder at that, for we that have studied the Italian opera may do anything in this kind."

"Pyramus and Thisbe," a mock opera, set to music by Mr. Lampe, 1745, appears to be the same as the preceding, judging from a comparison of it with the description of Leveridge's piece.

At Drury Lane, February 3, 1755, was acted a new English opera called "The Fairies." This piece, which is in three acts and which was produced nine times, is usually attributed to Garrick. The dialogue is compiled from "A Midsummer Night's Dream," and about twenty-seven songs are added. The clowns are omitted and consequently the episode of Titania's love for Bottom. The parts of Lysander and Hermia were taken by two Italians, whom Wilkinson says were of great service, whereat Genest exclaims, "'Midsummer Night's Dream' turned into an opera and assisted by two foreigners must have been a blessed exhibition, and highly to the credit of Garrick, who talked so much of his zeal for Shakespeare!"

Another bad alteration of this play was performed at Drury Lane, November 23, 1763. This time it was turned into a sort of opera with thirty-three songs, nearly the whole of the mock play being discarded. As usual, much of the original dialogue is omitted. "This alteration," says Genest, "was attributed originally to Colman, but it seems to have been made by Garrick, Colman, at his desire, having only superintended the rehearsals." It was unsuccessful, a second performance not being given.

"A Fairy Tale," in two acts, 1763, is apparently an abridgment of the preceding. Act I, scene 1, is "Midsummer Night's Dream," I, 2, a song with an introduction and comments being added. Scene 2 is II, 1, much shortened, with songs introduced. One song is made up of the description of Robin Goodfellow's deeds as given in Shakespeare, put in song measure. Scene 3 is from II, 2 (the fairy part). The first scene of Act II is III, 1, abridged. Puck is represented as driving off by a storm the "mechanicals" turned actors, the episode of the ass's head being omitted. Scene 2 has a little of III, 2, and is very short, ending with the four-line song "Up and down, Up and down," etc. Scene 3 is from IV, 1, with a duet and songs, one from "Henry VIII" (the first verse of "Orpheus with his lute," etc.), and one a version of "Sigh no more," etc., from "Much Ado," which runs as follows:

> "Sigh no more, lady, sigh no more,
> Be not inconstant ever,
> One foot on sea, and one on shore,
> You can be happy never."

Merchant of Venice

One of the most flagrant instances of literary crime is the version of this play perpetrated by George Granville, Lord Lansdowne, and called by him "The Jew of Venice." It appeared in 1701, and held the stage to the entire supplantation of Shakespeare's play until 1741, when Macklin gave his celebrated performance of the original. Even then, although it had received its deathblow, it died a lingering death, for some little time, indeed, apparently holding its own with the original. This fact is a sad reflection on the taste of the theatre-going public of that day.

In his "Advertisement to the Reader," Lansdowne justifies his undertaking by the examples of the great men who have preceded him in the same kind of enterprise. "Besides many others too numerous to mention," he cites Waller, the Earl of Rochester, the Duke of Buckingham, D'Avenant, Dryden, Shadwell, and Tate. From his point of view, surely here was ample justification, but we of a later day and, in some respects we hope, a wiser literary generation, will not be so impressed as he with the weight of his exemplars.

The play is provided with a prologue written by his friend Bevill Higgons, Esquire, which consists of a dialogue between the laurel-crowned ghosts of Shakespeare and Dryden. After some mutual commendation and some regret for the depraved taste which prefers farces to their scenes, the ghost of Shakespeare is made, rather curiously, to utter the sentiments of Mr. Higgons as to this play and its author, and to speak of himself in the third person.

> " The scenes in their rough native dress were mine,
> But now improved with nobler lustre shine;
> The first rude sketches Shakespeare's pencil drew,
> But all the shining masterstrokes are new.
> This play, ye critics, shall your fury stand,
> Adorned and rescued by a faultless hand."

We wonder at the blindness of a man who could write such a prologue and at the vanity of a man who could listen to its recitation as an introduction to his play.

There is no change in plot in the First Act. The first scene is curtailed considerably and the diction is changed unnecessarily and arbitrarily as is usual throughout the play. The second scene is rewritten, only three suitors being described, M. le Compte, the Frenchman, Myn Heer Van Gutts, a Dutchman, who is substituted for the German of the original, and the Englishman, who is dismissed without detailed characterization, as he is "the Frenchman's ape" and "an ape of an ape must needs be a strange monster." The consideration of the Dutchman as a possible husband by Portia furnishes Lansdowne with the opportunity to make her utter this refinement, "La Signora Gutts! Oh hideous! What a sound would there be in the mouth of an Italian!" The third scene is about as in Shakespeare, but is somewhat abridged.

Act II is much changed. The princes of Morocco and Arragon are omitted entirely, a practice which later acting versions have generally adopted. Old Gobbo, Launcelot, Salarino, Salanio, and Tubal are also rejected. These omissions bring it about that Lansdowne's Second Act commences with the line, "I am bid forth to supper, Jessica," in the 5th scene of Act II of Shakespeare's play. It follows the original until Shylock's exit; Jessica's two lines are increased to seven; then enter Lorenzo and Gratiano, and the elopement takes place. Great changes are made in the dialogue. The next scene is new, and consists of an "Entertainment" at Bassanio's. The only indebtedness to Shakespeare is for a few lines, Lorenzo's lines in praise of music from Act V being inserted here. Antonio, Shylock, and others are present and music is played. The characters drink toasts. Friendship is proposed by Antonio; love and Portia by Bassanio; the sex in general by Gratiano; and then Shylock gives a toast to his "mistress that outshines them all," "money," "interest upon interest," which he alone drinks. This is followed by a masque of about one hundred and fifty lines, called "Peleus and Thetis," which his lordship doubtless felicitated himself greatly upon and regarded as ample compensation for the omitted portions of the original. Here again we feel compelled to differ with him. After the masque, Bassanio takes farewell of Antonio, the master of the ship having sent two servants to desire Bassanio to come aboard. This is mostly from Shakespeare, Antonio, however, speaking the lines that in the original Salarino quotes to Salanio as his.

Act III begins with the casket scene of Bassanio's choosing, which is altered somewhat by the addition of borrowings from the two omitted casket scenes of Act II. The parts of Gratiano and Nerissa are enlarged, but the latter part of the scene follows Shakespeare, aside from a few omissions and verbal changes and from the fact that at the very end Lorenzo's lines to Portia from the fourth scene are inserted. Scene 2 is a combination of Shakespeare's III, 3, and III, 1. It is laid in a Venetian jail, opens like III, 3, and is like that scene for the most part. The familiar passage beginning "To bait fish withal," is put in as the answer to Antonio's question, "Thou wilt not take my flesh; what's that good for?" Then follow some prosaic and commonplace lines of Lansdowne's, in which Shylock is made to lament that he cannot recover the jewels and ducats that Jessica has taken, and to tell Antonio that he (Antonio) shall pay for all.

Act IV has no great variation from the original, as to the action, but the changes of diction and in the conception of the different characters as indicated by their speeches and acts have so transformed or, rather, transmogrified the trial scene as to detract greatly from, if not altogether to remove, its dignity. Portia finally, when she finds Shylock to be merciless, throws aside her judicial decorum to display a violent partisanship, even descending to offensive utterances.

Shylock, who throughout the play has been debased and made a thoroughly vulgar, money-loving Jew, a striking contrast to Shakespeare's tragic figure, in whom is concentrated the wrath, malignity, and thirst for vengeance of a race in which centuries of oppression and persecution have fostered and developed these feelings to an extreme, laughs derisively at the exhibition of friendship on the part of Antonio and Bassanio. To the last are unsuitably transferred the sarcastic counter-comments of Gratiano; he seeks to interfere with the apparent course of justice by offering to sacrifice himself and by drawing to defend Antonio, the effect of all of which modification is a decided loss of dignity. Indeed, the whole scene as altered by Lansdowne is crude and inartistic in comparison with Shakespeare's. After Shylock's condemnation, Portia asks Bassanio for the ring, which he withholds, although making no mention of its having been the gift of his wife. This is because the reference to the marriage ceremony had been omitted from the casket scene.

Act V does not differ greatly from the original, except for changes in the diction. Bassanio, however, is represented as momentarily angry at Antonio, to whom he attributes his loss of the ring, and Portia claims to have obtained it by art magic, which gives to Bassanio the opportunity of uttering fifteen lines or so of twaddle on that subject.

Such is the work of the "faultless hand" which "improved" Shakespeare's scenes.

About the only commendation that can be given to the author of this travesty is the very negative praise that is involved in saying that he did not go so far in his ill use of Shakespeare as some of his predecessors and successors in this same field, as, notably, those whom he cites as examples. The features that merit condemnation and arouse indignation, on the contrary, are many, but only a few of them are worth notice or mention. The changes are invariably for the worse and greatly so. In place of the good comedy furnished by Launcelot and Old Gobbo, we are given the tedious, inane, and absolutely uninspired masque. In the reconstruction of the casket scenes, the lessening of the number of which may be justified as an exigency of time, our author has mutilated some of the best lines and passages, and there is wretched botching exhibited also in the Third Act, in which scenes had to be run together because of the omission of characters.

The chief feature of interest in this version is the perverted conception of the character of Shylock. It seems strange to us that any normal person could regard the Shylock of Shakespeare as any but a highly tragic part. But apparently Lansdowne did so, or, if he did not, he thought the characterization would be improved by making the Jew more contemptible. At any rate, it must be conceded that he is successful in his persistent endeavor to lower Shylock and has rendered him altogether despicable. We become thoroughly disgusted with a Shylock who drinks a toast to his mistress, money, and who grins like an ape in the trial scene. What a striking contrast to a Shylock exalted by his wrath and desire for vengeance into an object of pity! Yet Lansdowne's Jew was for forty years the only Shylock with which theatregoers were familiar. Now and then a person might be found, like Rowe, who ventured the opinion that Shakespeare intended a different interpretation; but it was not until Macklin secured for himself eternal honor by lifting the character out of the slough into which it had fallen up to the firm ground of tragedy, or gave us, as Pope is said to have put it, "the Jew that Shakespeare drew," that the light dawned and Shakespeare's art came to be recognized. Along with the depression of Shylock appears an attempt to make Bassanio more prominent and estimable which has also, as carried out, resulted in debasing the character. Certainly our admiration for him is not increased by having him represented as getting angry with the friend who has done so much for him, or by his greater and unbecoming activity in the trial scene.

Leaving the action and coming to the diction, we find matter for as great if not greater censure, for Lansdowne, besides omitting many fine lines and passages of the original, in pursuing his purpose of "refining," changes the phraseology of what is retained, invariably for the worse, and adds much prosaic verse of his own composition. Grateful are we that this perversion is consigned to a well-merited oblivion.

As You Like It

This charming comedy was first altered by Charles Johnson, who, for the sake of a more significant title, called his version "Love in a Forest." Johnson, who was a tavern-keeper as well as a writer of plays, and who as a poetaster of the time is said to be mentioned in one of the versions of the "Dunciad," dedicated the printed copies of his play to the Worshipful Society of Freemasons, of which he was evidently an enthusiastic member. The play, when acted in 1723, met with no success and was withdrawn after six performances. Strangely enough, its original seems to have been entirely unknown to the stage of the period, for there is no record of its representation after the Restoration until 1740, when it was

acted about twenty-five times at Drury Lane. This
fact makes all the more laudable Johnson's desire, as
expressed in his prologue, of restoring to the stage
one more of Shakespeare's plays, and had he been
content with this and not have deemed it necessary to
revise Shakespeare for the purpose, we should have
been much indebted to him. But unfortunately his
judgment was at fault and he stultified himself by his
declaration that he had " refined his [Shakespeare's]
ore," " weeded the beautiful parterre," and " restored
the scheme from time and error."

Behold the result of the refining, weeding, and
restoring processes! Touchstone, Audrey, William,
Corin, and Phœbe are removed root and branch. Sil-
vius appears only in Act II, scene 4, where he speaks
about twenty lines given to Corin in the original.
How the deficiency thus created is made up will be
seen in the course of the account of the play, which
follows.

The first two acts are not greatly changed. A
ludicrous modification is that of the wrestling bout
to a combat in the lists, before beginning which
Charles and Orlando defy each other with the
speeches of Bolingbroke and Norfolk in " Richard
the Second," I, 1. Jacques himself reports his moralizing on the deer, a change approved by Genest but
criticised by Furness as " obliterating one of Shakespeare's artistic touches, whereby an important character is described and the keynote struck before he
himself appears."

More considerable changes appear in the Third
Act. The verses which Celia ought to read are
omitted, and she makes the comments and verses
given to Touchstone in Shakespeare's play. After
Orlando and Jacques enter, the chief change in the

play is instituted, namely, the wooing of Celia by Jacques. This is done in the words of Touchstone to Audrey, patched with some speeches of Benedick's from "Much Ado," the whole dialogue being given an eighteenth-century tone. This "monstrous device," curiously enough, anticipates George Sand's French version of the play, *Comme Il Vous Plaira,* but the coincidence is undoubtedly a mere accident, as it is not likely she had read Johnson's play.

The Fourth Act opens with a conversation in which Jacques tells Rosalind of his love for Celia. Viola's speech, "She never told her love," etc., is inserted in the scene between Rosalind and Orlando. It is Robert Du Bois who brings Rosalind Orlando's excuse for not keeping his promise, and he is the brother who is rescued from the lioness. Oliver is reported as having made away with himself to escape punishment, thus making Orlando his father's heir. Of course, the changes already made affect the dénouement somewhat, but the play ends substantially as in Shakespeare, except that Jacques marries Celia. To compensate for the omitted portions, the burlesque play of "Pyramus and Thisbe" from "A Midsummer Night's Dream" is dragged in, being represented before the Duke during the interval between the exit of the disguised Rosalind and her return in her true character.

Johnson's chief purposes appear to have been to give the play greater unity of action by limiting the action to fewer characters and to improve the characterizations of the chief persons. In carrying out the first design, he has deprived us of some of the best of the original; how lamentably he has failed in the second is almost too obvious from the foregoing account of his strange changes to need comment.

What shall be said of the transformation of the melancholy Jacques into an eighteenth-century lover? It is certainly most remarkable. One of Shakespeare's most distinctive characters, a universal favorite nowadays, is to our minds thereby entirely spoiled. Nothing but a complete failure to comprehend the great dramatist's purpose or ignorance of true dramatic art could have brought about such a perversion. The comedy is, as Furness points out, so thoroughly English that it cannot be transplanted to German or French soil. The Germans cannot appreciate the sparkling wit and vivacity of Rosalind, and consequently turn to Jacques and Touchstone as the leading characters. How it strikes a French mind may be learned from an examination of Sand's *Comme Il Vous Plaira,* in which Jacques is made the hero, being converted from a misogynist into a jealous lover, almost provoked to a duel with Orlando by Celia's coquetry. Johnson's mind seems to have undergone a sort of Frenchification, if one may so speak, the process being checked, however, before it was completed, so that he did not carry the change in the characterization of Jacques so far as his French successor. At any rate, both, it will be admitted, have debased the character most effectually. Perhaps the best criticism on the transformed Jacques is that which Johnson makes Celia herself utter: "Jacques's love looks a little awkward; it does not sit so easy on him." We should, however, amend it by making the language stronger. The omission of Touchstone and Audrey deprives us of some of the most delightful comedy to be found anywhere, and that of Corin and Phœbe lowers the characterization of Rosalind somewhat by doing away with her desire to make a lover happy by using her good offices in his behalf.

Another useless and very bad change is the removal of Oliver and the substitution of Robert as the brother rescued by Orlando. This was made necessary by the change in the lover of Celia. Perhaps, also, Johnson had in mind poetical justice, which would be, in his opinion, better satisfied by having Oliver take his own life. But how much it injures the conception of Orlando, besides removing one of the chief teachings of the play, the lesson of forgiveness, to take away from him the opportunity to show his magnanimity in preserving and forgiving an enemy! We must admit that Oliver's conversion is a little sudden, the great dramatist being undoubtedly influenced not a little by the dramatic convention which called for a pairing off of the chief characters in the fifth act. Nevertheless, one gets a fresh admiration for Shakespeare's genius, in observing his method of "making earthly things even," as compared with that of his uninspired reviser.

A greater Johnson has lamented that Shakespeare lost the opportunity for a fine piece of moralizing, in not recording the conversation between the usurping duke and the hermit. Fortunately, this idea did not occur to his lesser namesake, for which we may be grateful.

The dialogue, when Shakespeare is followed, is not greatly altered, but of course Johnson's changes and omissions make necessary much of his own composition. As a concluding word, it may be affirmed that this version is an extremely bad transformation of Shakespeare's most charming comedy. As we have seen, it was the opinion even of Johnson's contemporaries that his play was not good.

The Old Variorum list includes another alteration, "The Modern Receipt, or a Cure for Love.

OF SHAKESPEARE 79

A Comedy, altered from Shakespeare, 12mo, 1739." The dedication is signed " J. C." I was unable to get any information about it further than this, as I did not find a copy, and there is no mention of it in Genest.

The Taming of the Shrew

Another pleasing comedy that has suffered violence at the hands of revisers and adapters is " The Taming of the Shrew," as besides being altered, it has been resorted to for material for farces and afterpieces.

The chief alteration is so unique as to be well worth some attention. Here again there is a change of title, but in this case it is a much more violent one. Indeed, were the original title not appended as a sub-title to the altered play, the disguise would be complete. " Sauny the Scot, or the Taming of the Shrew," is one of the earliest versions of Shakespeare, for it was first acted in April, 1667, although not printed until 1698. It is attributed, with much probability, to the actor Lacy, though Langbaine in his account of dramatic writers does not speak of it as his. Lacy himself took the part of Sauny, who is Grumio turned into a Scotchman. The play met with considerable success, although Pepys, who records seeing it, thought it " generally but a mean play " with " some very good pieces in it."

The scene of the play is transferred to London, the dialogue is shortened and converted into prose, and the Fifth Act is almost entirely new. Petruchio remains as in the original, but the names of most of the other dramatis personæ are changed. Katharine becomes Margaret, daughter of Lord Beaufoy

(Baptista). In Winlove, son of Sir Lionel Winlove and a country gentleman of Oxford education, may be recognized Lucentio, now become an Englishman; Gremio, Hortensio, and Biondello become respectively Woodall, a rich old citizen, Geraldo, and Jamy. The character of Sauny is much more important than that of Grumio in Shakespeare's play. He is Petruchio's Scotch servant and a mere buffoon. Curiously enough, his language, which is often coarse, is not Scotch in its idiom or apparent pronunciation, but Yorkshire dialect. Margaret and Petruchio talk like people of the London streets.

The Induction is omitted, not a bad change as its representation is unnecessary. The First Act is very short, consisting of Shakespeare's first scene only. The second scene of Act I, and the whole of Act II constitute Lacy's Second Act. Sauny figures very prominently in this act. Act III consists of Shakespeare's Third Act with the first two scenes of his Fourth Act. Winlove (Lucentio) speaks a kind of French English. Petruchio makes Margaret smoke. Snatchpenny, a London thief, has the part of the pedant. The remainder of Act IV and the first scene of Act V of the original make up Lacy's Fourth Act. Woodall is represented as hiring Winlove, as a Frenchman, to woo Bianca for him. Act V, as has been said, is almost entirely Lacy's, although the wager on the wives' obedience is introduced. It consists mainly in a prolongation of Margaret's resistance to Petruchio. He declares her to be dead and orders his servants to carry her out and bury her. The wager episode follows and then the play ends with a dance.

It will be seen that the play has thus been transformed into a low comedy or into a mere farce. The change of scene has been attended with a marked lowering of the whole tone of the play and a striking degradation of the chief characters. For this the little good humor that has been added is far from compensating, much less does it excuse it. The prolongation of Margaret's stubbornness, while perhaps good fooling, certainly cannot be called an improvement or even a welcome addition. Shakespeare knew when to stop.

On the whole, the play, although bad enough as an alteration of Shakespeare, is still a fairly good play, because so much of the original is retained. There was no call to change the setting and to degrade the play. This and the destruction of the poetry are the chief features to be condemned. It is only one more proof of the lack of anything like reverence for Shakespeare among the playwrights and audiences of the period, that such a version could be made and, moreover, be tolerated, let alone be received with applause, as it was.

The two farces (1716), based upon the Induction and called "The Cobbler of Preston," one by the actor Christopher Bullock and the other by Charles Johnson, whose acquaintance we have made before as the author of "Love in a Forest," do not deserve much more than a mention. The former was composed to offset the production of the latter at a rival theatre and is said to be on the whole the better, or probably one should say the latter is the worse and not infer that either possessed any excellence. According to Genest, Johnson's farce is merely founded on Shakespeare, contains political allusions directed against the Jacobites, and is managed badly in that the trick is played on Sly a second time. Bullock's is less bad in that he uses some of the language of the original, abstains from political allusions, and manages the deception of Sly better. The only thing that impressed me in reading it was its exceeding coarseness.

I shall have to rely again upon Genest, to whom so many times I am indebted, for my account of "A Cure for a Scold," a ballad opera, which comes next in order of time. It is by Worsdale, a portrait painter, and was given in 1735 as an afterpiece at a performance of "Richard III." The author professes to have founded his piece on Shakespeare's play, but in reality he has stolen the greater part from "Sauny the Scot," either verbatim or with slight changes. Manly, Archer, and Peg correspond respectively to Petruchio, Grumio, and Katharine of Shakespeare's play.

Garrick cut Shakespeare's play down to a three-act farce in 1756, by omitting the characters of Vincentio, Tranio, and Lucentio and much of the dialogue. He called the adaptation "Katharine and Petruchio." It opens with Petruchio's telling Baptista of his intention to woo the latter's daughter, and, with some unimportant omissions and additions, follows Act II of the original. The Second Act begins with III, 1, and ends with IV, 2. The dialogue is made up of passages in the main judiciously selected. The last act consists of the remainder of the play similarly treated. Some of the good speeches or lines of the discarded characters are retained and transferred.

There is nothing of importance to our subject in this. Garrick, who has in this case shown greater wisdom than is usual in his adaptations of Shakespeare, has certainly produced a most excellent afterpiece, but no great credit can be given him for degrading a good comedy into a farce, even though it is an excellent one. The change of title was unnecessary, and Kemble, in revising Garrick's piece later, restored the original title.

CHAPTER V. ALL'S WELL THAT ENDS WELL — TWELFTH NIGHT — THE WINTER'S TALE — KING JOHN — RICHARD II — 1 HENRY IV — 2 HENRY IV

All's Well that Ends Well

THIS play was altered by a Mr. Pilon and reduced to three acts in 1785. His version was never printed and I could learn nothing as to its nature.

Twelfth Night, or, What You Will

"Love Betrayed, or the Agreeable Disappointment," 1703, by Charles Burnaby, is a comedy based upon "Twelfth Night." According to Genest, about fifty lines are professedly taken from Shakespeare's play, and the plot and incidents come from the same source. The dialogue is written afresh, but, says Genest, "This comedy is rather to be considered as a very bad alteration of Shakespeare's play than as a new one." I did not find a copy of Burnaby's production, so, of course, I cannot testify as to the truth or falsity of the stage historian's remark.

The Winter's Tale

Several alterations or adaptations of this play or of a part of it have been made. The first is a reconstruction of the last two acts of Shakespeare's play into a dramatic pastoral centering about the sheepshearing scene. It is attributed to M'Namara Morgan, author of an uninspired tragedy called "Philoclea," founded on Sidney's "Arcadia," and was produced at Covent Garden, March 25, 1754, as an afterpiece. It is in two acts and opens with a scene in verse founded on IV, 1, in which Polixenes tells Camillo of his son's attachment to a shepherdess and adds that he does not object to his having an intrigue with her, but only to his marrying her. Next follows IV, 3, and then comes a scene, mostly new, in which the king and Camillo, on their way to the sheepshearing, inquire the way of Autolycus. Act II is the sheepshearing scene somewhat altered. Perdita sings a song. After Polixenes has discovered himself and expressed his determination to break off the match, the old shepherd, who very conveniently turns out to be Antigonus, informs the king that the maiden is daughter to Leontes. Of course Polixenes is then reconciled to his son, and the piece thereupon ends with a song by Autolycus.

This production is objectionable in a number of respects. First and foremost, in principle, as an undignified use of Shakespeare's play and material, secondly in that the author associated too much of his own invention with the dialogue he takes from the original, especially in the part of Autolycus, and thirdly in the debasement of the character of Polixenes indicated by his remark to Camillo.

About two years later, to be precise, on January 21, 1756, Garrick's alteration was acted at Drury Lane, together with his alteration of "The Taming of the Shrew," "Katharine and Petruchio." This time the piece was an expansion of Shakespeare's last two acts into three acts by adding some new portions and taking over matter from the first three acts of the original. Act I, 1, is partly IV, 1, with additions summarizing the events of the previous acts of Shake-

86 ALTERATIONS AND ADAPTATIONS

speare's play. Leontes is said to be coming to "Bithynia" again. Scene 2 is at first from III, 3, from "Enter an old shepherd," but Leontes and Cleomenes are rescued from shipwreck instead of the child. Scene 3 is IV, 2.

Act II, 1, is like IV, 3, down to "Enter a servant," save that Perdita's song from Morgan's play is introduced. Leontes and Cleomenes are present as spectators. After Polixenes and Camillo, the latter of whom has, of course, never changed his allegiance, go out, Leontes offers his assistance to Florizel toward reconciling the prince to his father, which favor Florizel accepts. Genest says in criticism of this feature, "If Garrick was determined to make use of this expedient for detaining Florizel at home, he ought to have made Leontes declare who he really was, as it is very unnatural for Florizel to place any reliance on the mediation of a stranger, notwithstanding the mysterious hints of his being of more consequence than he seemed to be."

Act III, 1, begins with the soliloquy of Autolycus and follows Shakespeare closely. Scene 2 is new. A gentleman tells Paulina of the arrival of Leontes, his reconciliation to Polixenes, and his intercession for Florizel. To them enters Camillo, who tells of the reconciliation and of the joy which has come in the discovery that Perdita is the long-lost daughter of Leontes. Paulina speaks of the statue of Hermione that she wishes the king to see. Scene 3 is V, 2, from "Exeunt gentlemen." Scene 4 is the scene at Paulina's house, part of V, 1, being combined with V, 3, with some changes.

Although Garrick's additions are far from the standard of the original and his changes and his borrowings from the omitted acts are often injudicious and result in mutilating Shakespeare's play, and although, further, this is irreverent treatment on his part of the great master whom he professed to admire so much, his play proved acceptable and was revived from time to time during that century. Its influence even passed into the next century, for Kemble in reviving "The Winter's Tale" in 1802 at Drury Lane, adopted Garrick's additions or modifications in a few instances.

This pleasing romantic comedy was in 1756 printed as altered by Charles Marsh, a bookseller and a friend of Garrick's, who revised three or four of Shakespeare's plays, but who never succeeded in getting his productions of this kind acted and did not venture to print all of them. This alteration was published at the time that Garrick's adaptation was being acted at Drury Lane. Marsh appears to have borne no little resentment against the manager for his preferring his own piece to his friend's. The title page has the following address to Garrick:

> " Think'st thou the Swan of Avon spreads her wings,
> Her brooding wings for thee alone to plume
> And nestle there, O Garrick? — Thou deserv'st
> Indeed, much cherishing; thy melody
> Charms ev'ry ear. But sure, it ill beseems
> One cygnet, thus to stretch its little pinions,
> Ambitiously intent, to fill that nest
> Whose roomy limits well may shelter numbers."

The sixteen elapsed years was the special rock which our dramatic mariner wished to avoid. Such a grave breach of the sacred unity of time was not to be tolerated. Garrick and Morgan had subjected the play to an heroic treatment to overcome the difficulty and had rejected the first three acts *in toto*, remodeling what was left according to their pleasure. Marsh, however, preferred, beside following their example with respect to the last two acts, to rewrite largely the foregoing portion, in such a way as to do away with the long wait. He also obviated the distressing geographical error involved in the "coast of Bohemia," by adopting Hanmer's change of Bohemia to Bithynia.

Marsh's play begins then at the time when Shakespeare's Fourth Act begins. His first scene is a new one (there are occasional lines from Shakespeare), in which Alcidales and Rogero, two Sicilian lords, converse about the unfortunate Leontes's long jealousy and the sixteen years imprisonment his queen has undergone. In scene 2, the king has joined them. The first part of the scene is like II, 3, down to "Enter Paulina with a child;" then follows part of I, 2, the speeches of Camillo, who, of course, had long been in banishment, being transferred to the two lords. There is much additional. The two lords give it as their opinion that the supposed guilty persons are innocent, and the king tells of sending to the oracle. Then Paulina enters, though, of course, without the child, and the remainder is partly like II, 3. Antigonus is, however, absent, as he has long been gone. Paulina tells the king that Antigonus has appeared to her in a dream and has told her that he left Leontes's babe on Bithynia's shore and that she comes at Hermione's desire to ask that the question of the latter's innocence or guilt may be determined by an impartial test of justice. If not proved innocent, the queen desires to be condemned to death, a fate which she prefers to imprisonment. The king replies, "Apollo, judge between us," and then comes in a messenger announcing the return of those who have been sent to consult the oracle. The king orders a court to be held.

Act II, scene 1, is like III, 1. Scene 2 is a new one and is laid in the prison, a little of it being taken from II, 2. Paulina is with Hermione. The queen is rejoicing in the opportunity to have her innocence established and thanks the faithful Paulina for her efforts in her friend's behalf. Scene 3 is III, 2. Shakespeare's third scene is necessarily omitted.

The rest of the play follows the original pretty closely. Marsh's Third Act is made up of IV, 1, IV, 2, and part of IV, 3. Act IV is the remainder of IV, 3, with some additions. Act V is like Shakespeare's.

This and the other treatments of this play were, as is sufficiently obvious, undertaken in the interest of the unity of time. Even the most liberal of the pseudo-classicists could not, as has been said, condone so flagrant a violation of this principle as Shakespeare has committed in this play. But the romantic drama, in which perfect freedom was allowed and in which this "rule of art" was not consciously observed, exhibits not uncommonly lapses of time even far greater. In Lyly's "Endymion," for instance, forty years are supposed to intervene between the time when Endymion falls asleep and the return of Eumenides with his news. We who are not enslaved by the rules of pseudo-classicism and who accept the spirit and method of the romantic drama regard the lapse of time between acts as a perfectly legitimate dramatic convention and the representation of two, perhaps widely sundered, periods in the life of persons as natural and proper in a drama. Moreover in this case it was necessary to the dramatic purpose, which was to exhibit that "triumph of time" (as

Greene's subtitle to his story which was the source of Shakespeare's play has it), by which all is turned to good however man may err.

Believing as we do that Shakespeare's handling of the subject is natural and artistic, we must utterly condemn those efforts to remove the infraction of the unity of time which resulted in the cases of Morgan's, Garrick's, and Colman's pieces in the omission of many fine scenes and passages of the play, and in the case of the play just described in the mingling of so much of the reviser's poetry with Shakespeare's. The result is the same in every case; the play is spoiled to a great extent.

It made not the slightest difference to Shakespeare whether Bohemia had a sea coast or not or that Delphos was not on an island. Even if he knew Greene to be wrong on these points, he probably thought it not worth while to correct them. We agree with him and have no patience with the attempts to remedy the difficulties, either by substituting some other country or as, in the case of Bohemia, by finding justification for his making that country a maritime one. It is far too trivial to raise such a pother about.

There remains to be noticed another dramatic pastoral called "Sheepshearing," which was given at the Haymarket in 1777, being acted, however, only once. The compiler, who is supposed to be Colman, professed to take the piece from Shakespeare, but in fact it is an abridgment of Garrick's version. The visit of Leontes to Bohemia is retained, together with some other of Garrick's uninspired additions. Florizel sings two songs and the play ends with a song borrowed from Morgan's play.

The Life and Death of King John

Colley Cibber, dramatist, theatre manager, actor, poet laureate, and hero of the Dunciad, besides being the author of one of the most famous of the alterations of Shakespeare — I refer to his " Richard III " — is also responsible for another revision, which, unlike the earlier work, had a very short run and is now known only to dramatic history.

"Papal Tyranny in the Reign of King John" was the title he gave to his production — the reason for the amended title will soon appear — and the play was first given at Covent Garden, February 15, 1745. It had been offered for representation and put into rehearsal nine years before, but Cibber, angry because he was criticised for again presuming to meddle with Shakespeare, went to the playhouse secretly and carried away the play. It is to this occurrence that Pope alludes in the " Dunciad " in the line " King John in silence modestly expires." When, however, the nation was threatened by a Popish pretender, Cibber's patriotism got the better of all personal considerations, and the drama was produced, the author himself returning to the stage to act the part of Pandulph. This play was opposed by the revival of the original at Drury Lane and was soon withdrawn.

Cibber's attitude will best be made evident by quoting from the dedication to the Earl of Chesterfield, prefixed to the printed copies: "In all the historical plays of Shakespeare," he declares, "is scarce any fact that might better have employed his genius than the flaming contest between his insolent Holiness and King John. This is so remarkable a passage in our histories that it seems surprising our Shakespeare should have taken no more fire at it. . . . It was this coldness then, my lord, that first incited me to inspirit his King John with a resentment that justly might become an English monarch, and to paint the intoxicated tyranny of Rome in its proper colors. And so far, at least, my labor has succeeded, that the additional sentiments which King John throws out upon so flagrant a provocation were received with those honest, cordial applauses which English auditors I foresaw would be naturally warmed to. My success in this point, which I had chiefly at heart, makes me almost unconcerned for what may be judged of the further mechanism of the play; I have endeavored to make it more like a play than what I found it in Shakespeare."

Cibber apparently did not know that he was returning to the harsh, anti-Romish spirit that characterized the old play that Shakespeare recast, and which, in recasting, he rejected.

The play opens with the scene before Angiers, the entire First Act of the original being omitted. There are two slight changes in the new First Act. It is Constance, instead of Faulconbridge, who suggests the combination of forces against the city, and the Abbot of Angiers, instead of the "First Citizen," who suggests the marriage to make peace between the kings.

In the Second Act, the dispute between King John and Pandulph is considerably enlarged, and it is here that Cibber takes the opportunity to express his sentiments regarding the Roman hierarchy. Another new feature is a short conversation between the Dauphin and Blanche about the unhappy breaking off of the negotiations.

There are many minor changes in the Third Act. The most noteworthy departures from Shakespeare

are in the scene between Hubert and Arthur. Nothing is said about proposing to put Arthur's eyes out, but he is to be killed with a dagger, after writing a statement that he has killed himself. After the keeper has spared the boy's life, he permits Constance, who has been captured, to have an interview, not represented in the play, with her son.

Act IV is much changed. It begins in the French camp near Bury. Pandulph describes the effect of his anathema, and a letter of submission is brought by Faulconbridge from King John. There are unimportant changes not a few.

In the last act, Salisbury stabs Hubert, who is present when Arthur's body is found. Many slight alterations are made and there is one considerable addition, that of the funeral of the prince at Swinstead Abbey, at which ceremony his mother is, rather improbably, represented as being present. The play ends with the death of the King and the leading off of Constance.

So badly is the play mangled that it may be said to be practically written afresh. Among the numerous changes, two stand out, the virtual disappearance of Faulconbridge and the enlargement of the character of Constance. By the former, one of Shakespeare's most individual and skilfully portrayed characters, whose words and actions constitute one of the best features of the play, is lost to us. To compensate for this deprivation, the latter change is made, which the author doubtless thought would be very acceptable to his audience. Probably this is one of the principal things that to Cibber's mind made the history "more like a play." That the woman element must be made an important one was, as we have seen, an article of the dramatic faith of the time.

It may be noted, in passing, that our author, in making Constance more prominent, has represented her as doing several things for which history affords no warrant, a practice which he adopts in many other cases. Anyone who reads this play will not long be uncertain as to the comparative excellence of Shakespeare and Cibber as playwrights and poets. Perhaps in no other scene will Cibber's lack of true dramatic art be more obvious than in that between King John and Hubert, which in Shakespeare is well-nigh perfect but which Cibber has completely spoiled. But nothing will be gained by a further discussion of this mangling process. It is much worse than in the version of " Richard III," and it is no wonder that the play quickly succumbed when brought into comparison with the production of the original at a rival theatre.

It is interesting and amusing to learn that the proprietor of Drury Lane Theatre advertised that he had put off the requested revival of Shakespeare's " King John," because Cibber had insinuated that this was likely to damage him, but that, " finding from the bills that ' Papal Tyranny ' was not an alteration of ' King John ' but a new tragedy on the same plan," he would not delay the exhibition.

Cibber's treatment of the dialogue will best appear from a brief quotation. Of course, he added a great deal of his own. Ten lines from the familiar passage at the opening of Shakespeare's Act III are reduced to six and robbed of most of their vigor:

> "A peace with England, and by France concluded!
> Affianced too! Blanch to the Dauphin married!
> And Arthur's ruin made her pompous dowry,
> Thou dost abuse my ear, it cannot be!
> I have a monarch's oath to right my cause,
> And 'twere to wrong thy master, to believe thee!"

OF SHAKESPEARE

Although Cibber's "King John" was short-lived as an acted play, its influence did not die, for as late as May 20, 1803, an alteration made by Doctor Valpy, originally for representation at Reading School, was given at Covent Garden. In this the compiler borrowed to some extent from Cibber and, like him, omitted the First Act and debased the character of Faulconbridge. Valpy also added much of his own and made many unnecessary changes in the diction, but he wisely did not venture to tamper with the great scenes.

That there were some people with taste enough to see the folly of the practice of attempting to improve Shakespeare, the following humorous dialogue will show. It was written by Fielding in his "Historical Register" for 1736, and was probably the chief cause of the anger which, as we have seen, made Cibber take away the play.

Enter GROUND IVY (Colley Cibber).

"*Ground Ivy.* What are you doing here?

Apollo. I am casting the parts in the Tragedy of King John.

Ground Ivy. Then you are casting the parts in a tragedy that will not do.

Apollo. How, sir! Was it not written by Shakespeare? And was not Shakespeare one of the greatest geniuses that ever lived?

Ground Ivy. No, sir. Shakespeare was a pretty fellow and said some things which only want a little of my licking to do well enough; King John as now writ will not do. But a word in your ear, I will make him do.

Apollo. How?

Ground Ivy. By alteration, sir; it was a maxim of mine, when I was at the head of theatrical affairs, that no play, tho' ever so good, would do without alteration."

Sourwit, a critic, ridicules the idea of Ground Ivy's altering of Shakespeare; to which Medley (Fielding himself) admirably replies: "As Shakespeare is already good enough for people of taste, he must be altered to the palates of those who have none; and if you will grant that, who can be properer to alter him for the worse?"

"*Sourwit.* I hope, sir, your Pistol is not intended to burlesque Shakespeare.

Medley. No, sir. I have too great an honor for Shakespeare to think of burlesquing him; and, to be sure of not burlesquing him, I will never attempt to alter him, for fear of burlesquing him by accident, as, perhaps, some others have done."

We can only wish that the sentiments of Medley had been generally held at this period and before and after it.

The Tragedy of King Richard II

None of the history plays and few of the other plays have, if we may base an opinion on numerical grounds, received so much attention from revisers as this. I have, however, not seen a copy of any of the four or five "Richard II's" described or mentioned in the various stage histories, so I shall have to depend for my descriptions on the invaluable Genest.

The first in point of time is Tate's alteration, which was acted under the name of "The Sicilian Usurper" at the Theatre Royal in 1681. It seems that the play was suppressed, first under its proper name, and then as disguised with the above title, the authorities condemning it without examination. It was not, however, regard or reverence for Shakespeare that brought this about, but political reasons. Tate complains bitterly of this treatment in his dedication, as he thought "it would have found protection from whence it received prohibition." "For the two days in which it was acted," he says, "the change of scene, names of persons, etc., was a great disadvantage. I have called my persons Sicilians, but might as well have made them inhabitants of the World in the Moon." Tate boasts that he has heightened the character of Richard and tried to palliate his miscarriages and adds, "the arbitrary courtiers of the reign here written scarcely did more violence to the subjects of those times than I have done to truth, in disguising their foul practices; every scene is full of respect to majesty, and the dignity of courts; not one altered page but what breathes loyalty." But we cannot pity Tate, for he has meanly disfigured Shakespeare's play for the sake of conciliating the persons in power.

Tate's additions are, as might be expected, absolutely uninspired and dull. The only commendable feature is that so much of the original has been retained. The most prominent change is in the characterization of York, who is debased to a comic character intended by Tate as a model of loyalty. He is faithful to Richard until that king is deposed, when he promptly transfers his allegiance to Bolingbroke, the new king.

We may conclude by saying that this is only another instance of the almost utter lack of reverence for Shakespeare, which characterized the time and justified the use of a play of his as a vehicle for political opinion.

Yet greater violence was done to Shakespeare by Lewis Theobald, the Shakespeare editor, whose version of "Richard II" was acted in 1719 at the theatre in Lincoln's Inn Fields. He was not at all indebted to Tate. In his preface he says: "I have made some innovations upon history and Shakespeare; as in bringing Richard and Bolingbroke to meet first at the Tower, keeping York steady to the interest of the King, heightening Aumerle's character in making him die for the cause, and in despatching Richard at the Tower, who, indeed, was murthered at Pontefract Castle. In these and such instances I think there may be reserved a discretionary power of variation, either for maintaining the unity of action, or supporting the dignity of the characters."

Theobald's attempt to make the play conform more nearly to the unities led him to omit, with the exception of some speeches which he has transposed, the First and Second Acts of the original, and to lay the scene the entire time at or before the Tower. To compensate for this omission he makes great additions of his own invention, the chief of which is a love intrigue between Aumerle and a new female character, Lady Percy, daughter of Northumberland. The lovers have two interviews, in the latter of which Aumerle, in taking out his handkerchief, drops a parchment which, after their departure, Northumberland reads, thereby discovering the conspiracy. Aumerle is executed in spite of York's pleading for him and Lady Percy's entreating her father to interfere in his behalf. Lady Percy then kills herself, and York, finding the king dead, also takes his own life. Bolingbroke concludes the play with a sentiment which would have come more properly from some other lips:

"Tho' vengeance may a while withhold her hand,
A king's blood, unatoned, must curse the land."

It will be readily seen that this attempt to make over the history according to the dramatic ideas of the time, to make it more like a play, as the customary phrase was, has resulted as usual in a bad mutilation of Shakespeare's play and in the production of a hodgepodge that is far, not only from being an improvement, but from being an equal, of the original. Moreover, the idea that the passion of love must figure prominently, which is responsible for the chief addition, has complicated the plot and thus in a measure worked against the unity of the play. Theobald by thus treating Shakespeare has done much to counterbalance the merits of his edition of the plays, and has made us not disposed to commiserate him for his castigation by the pen of Pope.

A third version of this play was made by one James Goodhall in 1772 and is said to be a very bad one. The "Biographia Dramatica" says that it was offered to Garrick, but did not meet with acceptance, and that it was printed at Manchester.

The "Biographia Dramatica" mentions another "Richard II" as acted at Bath in 1754 but never published. It was by Francis Gentleman, who was the author of "The Dramatic Censor," and who, according to the same authority, has the discredit of being the editor of the worst edition that has ever appeared of any English author, viz., Bell's Shakespeare (1774-75). Whether this was an alteration of Shakespeare's play or a new play on the same foundation is not stated.

The adaptation of "Richard II" first acted at Drury Lane, March 9, 1815, was in the main properly made. In one respect, however, the adapter, who was the actor Richard Wroughton, erred, and that was, in omitting too much of the original. For the rejected portions he substituted passages from other plays, such as " 2 Henry VI," " 3 Henry VI," " Anthony and Cleopatra," and " King Lear."

The First Part of King Henry IV

This play was printed in 1700 as revived at Lincoln's Inn Fields. On the title page it is said to be revised with alterations. This revision is attributed to Betterton and to him or whomever was the compiler great credit is due, as the only change is in the direction of judicious omission. Indeed, this adaptation is superior to modern acting versions in that it retains without curtailment the speeches of the Prince and Falstaff in the Second Act, when each assumes the character of the King, and also retains the character of Glendower, for the omission of which, as well as for the abridgment of the other scene, there is no good reason.

The Second Part of King Henry IV

The great success of Betterton's revival of " 1 Henry IV " induced him to revive the Second Part not long after. The revision was not printed, however, until after his death, and then was undated. In this instance he was not so happy as in the previous one, for he omitted much of the play and substituted for the omitted portions a considerable borrowing from " Henry V." To specify, he rejects I, 1, II, 3, III, 1, and V, 1, 2, and 4, and his Fifth Act is an abridgment of the First Act of " Henry V," to which is added the second scene of the Second Act of the same play. Praise is due him for not altering what he used, but we cannot justify him in making a patchwork of " 2 Henry IV " and " Henry V," or at least as an adaptation of " 2 Henry IV " cannot commend the play.

CHAPTER VI. HENRY V — 1, 2, AND 3 HENRY VI — RICHARD III — HENRY VIII — TROILUS AND CRESSIDA

The Life of King Henry V

THE only alteration of this play mentioned in the Old Variorum list is one by Kemble. As this was only with such omissions and transpositions as seemed necessary to fit the drama for the stage, it need not detain us.

Soon after the Restoration, the Earl of Orrery wrote a rimed play bearing the same title, but having no resemblance to Shakespeare's except in an historical way.

Aaron Hill, who was a poetaster and dramatist of considerable pretensions in his time, but who is now remembered chiefly for his kindness to Thomson when that poet came, unknown, to London, produced a play called "Henry the Fifth, or the Conquest of France by the English," which was acted at Drury Lane six times in the season of 1723-24, and was published with his other works.

Hill says in his preface to the reader: "The inimitable and immortal Shakespeare, about a hundred and thirty years since, wrote a play on this subject and called it the 'Life of King Henry the Fifth'; mine is new fabric, yet I built on his foundation; and the reader, I am afraid, will too easily discover without the help of a comparison in what places I am indebted to him."

Hill's play differs so entirely from Shakespeare's

that it cannot be called an alteration of it. It is rather a new play with borrowings. It is only interesting as showing how Frenchified the taste of its author and his times was. The comic element is entirely omitted, the scene is always in France, thus observing the unity of place more nearly, and much intrigue is introduced. The characters of the Dauphin and the Princess are amplified and a new character is introduced, Harriet, niece of Lord Scroop, whom Henry is said to have seduced and afterwards deserted, with the offer of a pension. She figures most prominently in the Fourth Act, when she is arrested on suspicion of treason and is brought before the King. She at first reproaches him for his desertion of her, but is soon pacified. She then gives him the Dauphin's letter and stabs herself. The King is supposed to have, some time before, visited France, under the assumed name of Owen Tudor, and to have seen the Princess, at which time she is represented to have fallen in love with him. She appears frequently in the play and in the Third Act learns that Owen Tudor is the King.

Hill seems to have read Orrery's play and to have taken a hint or two from it. He borrows, without regard to their sequence in the original, various passages from Shakespeare's play, but takes pains to spoil them by modification. It hardly need be said that the play is far inferior to Shakespeare's both as to plot and dialogue and well merits the oblivion into which it has fallen.

In a farce entitled "Half-pay Officers," given at Lincoln's Inn Fields, January 11, 1720, one of the characters was Fluellen and the part is about as in "Henry V." Two speeches are introduced from "Much Ado." Fluellen was a new character to many of the audience, as Shakespeare was not very much read at this period and his "Henry V" had not been acted since the Restoration.

The First Part of King Henry VI

This has not been altered.

The Second and Third Parts of King Henry VI

"Henry the Sixth, Part First, with the Murder of Humphrey Duke of Gloucester," 1681, by the Restoration dramatist John Crowne, is a bad alteration of this play. In the prologue we read:

> "Today we bring old gathered herbs 'tis true,
> But such as in sweet Shakespeare's garden grew.
> And all his plants immortal you esteem,
> Your mouths are never out of taste with him.
> Howe'er to make your appetites more keen,
> Not only oily words are sprinkled in;
> But what to please you gives us better hope,
> A little vinegar against the Pope."

The dedication is to Sir Charles Sedley, and in it Crowne says: "I called it in the prologue Shakespeare's play, though he has no title to the fortieth part of it. The text I took out of his 'Second Part of Henry the Sixth,' but as most texts are served, I left it as soon as I could. For though Shakespeare be generally very delightful, he is not so always. His volume is all uphill and down; Paradise was never more pleasant than some parts of it, nor Ireland and Greenland colder and more uninhabitable than others. And I have undertaken to cultivate one of the most barren places in it."

The declared purpose of the play is to expose to the people the follies of the Roman Catholic saints days, prayers, etc. Langbaine tells us that the play was opposed by the Popish faction, some members of which by their power at court got it suppressed; however, it was well received by the rest of the audience. In spite of the declaration of the dedication, Crowne's play is made up chiefly of the first four acts of " 2 Henry VI." It ends with the breaking out of Cade's Rebellion. Crowne has enlarged the parts of the Queen, Suffolk, and the Cardinal. Some scenes are rejected, as that containing the killing of Suffolk, while others are expanded, as that in which the Cardinal dies. There is also a scene dealing with the death of Gloucester. The unity of place is observed by making the action all take place at the Court of Westminster. Crowne sometimes follows Shakespeare's phraseology closely and sometimes modifies it greatly. He also makes great additions of his own. He has "sprinkled in" a great deal of "vinegar against the Pope," both by what he makes his characters say and by the hypocrisy with which he endows all the Roman Catholic ecclesiastics and their followers and agents.

Using the drama as a means of stirring up religious hatred, as was done in this case and was done later by Cibber in his " Papal Tyranny," is an abominable practice and can be excused only in the light of the unsettled condition of the times when these two plays appeared, times when the memory of plots and persecutions was still fresh and when Romish emissaries and intriguers were perniciously active. We are glad that Shakespeare was too generous-hearted to stoop to such dramatic felony. Crowne's play shows to disadvantage in this respect as in all others, and thus bears witness to his lack of taste and dramatic ability.

Crowne's "Henry the Sixth, Part Second, or the Misery of Civil War," 1681, takes up the history where the play just described leaves it, thus commencing with Cade's Rebellion. In spite of his statement in his prologue that, "The divine Shakespeare did not lay one stone," much is taken from that source either verbatim or with slight modification, although far less is borrowed than in the preceding play. Steevens observes that surely Shakespeare's works could have been but little read at a period when Crowne could venture such an assertion.

The chief additions made by Crowne are love scenes, which are numerous. Warwick makes love to Lady Grey in two scenes, in the latter of which she rejects him. Edward Plantagenet has an intrigue with a new female character, Lady Eleanor Butler, which gives occasion for several more love scenes. In the Fourth Act, after rejecting Warwick, Lady Grey marries Edward, who is bitterly reproached by Lady Eleanor for his desertion of her. In the Fifth Act, Lady Eleanor in boy's clothes is slain at the battle of Barnet by King Edward, who is ignorant of her identity.

This exhibits clearly and strikingly that treatment common to most of the alterations of the histories, the thrusting into them of amorous intrigues. The reason for this and its effect on the plays have been dealt with in the general discussion and criticism given earlier in the book, so that further notice of this feature would be superfluous here.

Ambrose Phillips ("Namby Pamby") wrote a dull declamatory tragedy called "Humphrey, Duke of Gloster," covering the same ground as "2 Henry

VI." He borrows about thirty lines from it, which fact he is careful to mention in his preface to the reader, in which he also indicates where they may be found.

Another bad alteration of the Second and Third parts of Henry VI was made by Theophilus Cibber, son of Colley Cibber, and represented in 1723. It bears the cumbersome title "An Historical Tragedy of the Civil Wars between the Houses of York and Lancaster in the Reign of King Henry Sixth," and deals with the same period as Crowne's Second Part, from which it borrows not a little. Love scenes between Prince Edward and Lady Anne, Warwick's daughter, are a new feature. Much more of Shakespeare is retained than is done in Crowne's plays, but as usual there is a good deal of the reviser's own. Genest conjectures that Cibber, who was then only twenty years old, had the assistance of Savage, with whom he was intimate, in writing such passages as are new.

"The Roses, or King Henry the Sixth," an historical tragedy given at Reading School in 1795, consists mainly of four acts, the first being excepted, of "3 Henry VI." It is by the principal, Doctor Valpy, who also adapted "King John" and (1802) "The Merchant of Venice," in the latter case by cutting out the last act. The scene is confined to England, to preserve as far as possible the unity of place, and the duration of the play is shortened. For the most part, the compiler uses Shakespeare's language; occasionally, however, he alters it slightly and adds some words or lines that are his own. Passages are transferred here from First and Second Henry VI and from "Richard II." The play was provided with an epilogue by that ludicrously prosaic and now forgotten poet laureate, Henry James Pye.

At Drury Lane, December 22, 1817, was acted "Richard, Duke of York, or the Contention of York and Lancaster," with Kean in the principal rôle. This play is compiled from the three parts of Henry VI, centering about the events which form the subject of the Second Part and especially the attempts of Richard to get the crown. It opens at the fourth scene of the Second Act of "1 Henry VI," and has a few scenes from this part in the First Act. The Second, Third, and Fourth Acts are all from "2 Henry VI," and the Fifth Act is made up of the First Act and the second scene of the Second Act of "3 Henry VI."

The main object of the compilation was to afford Kean the greatest opportunity in the part of the Duke of York, and for this reason the play ends without any conclusion of the history of Henry Sixth and is given the new name. The editor has most injudiciously and unnecessarily, as there was ample material in the three Shakespearean plays, put in passages from Chapman, Webster, and Marston, and also borrowed to a considerable extent from Crowne's Second Part to eke out the Cade scenes. Thus he has made an indifferent if not bad compilation.

The Tragedy of King Richard III

We have now come to probably the most famous of all the alterations of Shakespeare, Colley Cibber's "Richard III." This version, which was made in 1700, entirely supplanted the original and, as somewhat modified by J. P. Kemble in 1811, still keeps the stage. So firm has its hold become that it is said that even Edwin Booth thought it on the whole preferable to Shakespeare's play for stage purposes. When the original was revived at Covent Garden, March 12, 1821, it was looked upon as an alteration, we are told, and was received with scant favor. So the actors went back to Cibber. It is to Cibber, whose play the managers did not scruple to advertise as Shakespeare's, that we are indebted, as has been pointed out before, for the time-honored rants, "Richard's himself again!" and "Off with his head! So much for Buckingham!"

Cibber's changes consist largely in modification of the diction, in the omission of scenes of the original for which he substituted others of his own composition, and in changes in minor details of the action. The main plot is substantially retained. Cibber did not, like some others of his kind, introduce new characters or new love scenes, and for this forbearance he deserves great credit.

The nature and the extent of Cibber's revision and the relation of his play to Shakespeare's will best be seen when his play shall have been described.

The greater part of Shakespeare's First Act is omitted, only Gloster's soliloquy in the first scene and a few lines from another soliloquy of his in the second scene being retained. The scenes containing Clarence's dream and Queen Margaret's curses, two of the best features of the play, are excised. This, of course, necessitates large additions; so Cibber begins his play during the lifetime of Henry VI, and introduces a good deal from the last act of " 3 Henry VI," eking it out with passages from " 2 Henry IV " and " Richard II," and with not a little of his own invention. The scenes from " 3 Henry VI " are far inferior to the rejected ones of " Richard III."

Act II begins with an unimportant scene between

Tressel and Stanley. Scene 2 is like Shakespeare's I, 2, but Bedford's speech at the funeral of Henry V, which opens " 1 Henry VI," is added to Anne's part, and numerous minor changes are made. The third scene is Shakespeare's II, 2, shortened and much altered. In Cibber, Buckingham announces the death of King Edward to the Duchess of York. Shakespeare's II, 3, and II, 4, are omitted.

Cibber's III, 1 is like III, 1 of the original, but is rewritten and considerably abridged. As an example of Cibber's blundering, it may be mentioned that he so alters the dialogue as to make Gloster attempt to prove himself a bastard instead of his brother. Much of this act has disappeared. The second scene is made up of parts of III, 5, and III, 7, an interview between Anne and Gloster being added by Cibber.

Act IV, scene 1, is much altered from the corresponding scene in Shakespeare. It is improperly laid in the Tower instead of before it, and Queen Margaret is permitted to see the children and even to attempt to take them away, in spite of the fact that Richard had given orders that no one should be admitted. In Shakespeare, no one is admitted. Scene 2 is scene 2 of the original, cut down and badly altered. In this scene occur some ridiculous lines, which are worth quoting as an example of the stuff Cibber substituted for Shakespeare's verse:

> " I tell thee, coz, I've lately had two spiders
> Crawling upon my startled hopes. Now tho'
> Thy friendly hand has brushed 'em from me
> Yet still they crawl offensive to my eyes.
> I would have some friend to tread upon 'em."

Scene 3 is greatly modified. Tyrrel does not

soliloquize on the deaths of the princes, as they have not yet been murdered, but, instead, Dighton and Forrest are with him, and they are sent to perform the deed. Richard is given a soliloquy in which he seems to show some feeling of compunction. Tyrrel enters and reports the murder of the princes, and Richard orders him to put their bodies into a coffin full of holes, which is to be thrown into the Thames. A part of Shakespeare's scene 4 is incorporated with this scene. In the next scene, Cibber properly omits most of the long dialogue between the Queen and Gloster, but improperly rejects the part in which Richard, when informed of the coming of Richmond, gives hasty and contradictory orders. He leaves out other matter also that should have been retained.

Act V, scene 1, is Shakespeare's V, 2, with lines from IV, 5, V, 3, and "2 Henry VI." Scene 2 consists of a part of V, 3, with a few judicious changes, but with many unnecessary and several absurd ones. Scene 3 is made up of the remainder of the play. A number of lines are borrowed from "Henry V." Among other ridiculous changes, Richmond is made to rejoice at the coming of Elizabeth to congratulate him, whereas, in history, his marriage with her was reluctantly made for political reasons. Cibber had the sense to remove the difficulty of representation involved in having the ghosts address Richard and Richmond as if they were asleep within a short distance of each other.

Such is the mutilation of the great Elizabethan's play manufactured by Cibber, who, to crown all, himself acted the title part, for which his voice, it is said, unfitted him.

If Cibber had altered the play in the proper spirit in which such revisions should be made, he would have deserved our thanks, for the play is certainly susceptible of improvement in many minor points. But he was not content to do this, as we have seen, and, besides omitting much unnecessarily, resorted to the contemptible practice of constructing scenes out of passages from other plays. There was enough material in "Richard III" to make five acts without thus doing, for with its 3,620 lines, more than twice as many as the "Comedy of Errors" has, it is one of the very longest of Shakespeare's plays. But when, in addition to this, he wantonly and often absurdly modifies the diction and introduces so much of his own stuff, we can have only contempt for his performance. A few judicious changes he makes, it is true, but the credit for them is so overbalanced by the censure he deserves for those alterations that are for the worse, that it is almost lost sight of. It would be tedious and unprofitable to discuss the numerous minor changes in detail. The space and time it would take cannot be better occupied than by reproducing Hazlitt's criticism of the whole production. "In the patchwork 'Richard III' which is acted under the sanction of Shakespeare's name and which was manufactured by Cibber," he says, "some of the most important and striking passages in the principal characters have been omitted to make room for idle and misplaced extracts from other plays; the only intention of which seems to have been to make the character of Richard as odious and disgusting as possible. It is apparently for no other purpose than to make Gloster stab King Henry on the stage that the first abrupt introduction of the character in the opening of the play is lost in the tedious, whining morality of the uxorious king (taken from another play) — we say tedious, because it interrupts the business of the scene, and loses its beauty and effect by having no intelligible connection with the previous character of the mild, well-meaning monarch. The passages which the unfortunate Henry has to recite are beautiful and pathetic in themselves, but they have nothing to do with the world that Richard has to 'bustle in.' In the same spirit of vulgar caricature is the scene between Richard and Lady Anne (when his wife), interpolated without any authority, merely to gratify the favorite propensity to disgust and loathing. With the same perverse consistency, Richard, after his last fatal struggle, is raised up by some galvanic process, to utter the imprecation, without any motive but pure malignity, which Shakespeare has so properly put into the mouth of Northumberland on hearing of Percy's death. To make room for these worse than needless additions many of the most striking passages in the real play have been omitted by the foppery and ignorance of the prompt-book critics."

The Famous History of the Life of King Henry VIII

No alteration of this play appears ever to have been made.

Troilus and Cressida

Dryden, whose opinion of Shakespeare has been touched upon briefly in the general discussion of the subject, besides being concerned with D'Avenant in a most abominable alteration — or, rather, travesty — of "The Tempest," as we have seen, is responsible, this time solely so, for another remodeling of Shakespeare, namely, a version of this play, which he had produced at the Duke's Theatre in 1679. It bore the subtitle "Truth Found too Late," which indicates the great change in the dénouement of the play and in the characterization of the title characters. I have found no record of a representation of the original play after the Restoration, but Dryden's version was acted at intervals down to 1733. To the printed copies he prefixed a long preface, in the first part of which, after speaking of the reverence of his age for Shakespeare as far more just than that of the Grecians for Æschylus, he makes the remarks concerning Shakespeare's language and style, the substance of which has been given under the general discussion of the revisers' treatment of Shakespeare's diction. He thinks the play to be one of the author's earlier efforts, an opinion that modern scholarship has shown to be wrong. We are fortunate in having Dryden's own statement of his attitude and method of revision and cannot do better than to quote such parts of the preface as are relevant.

"For the play itself," he goes on to say, "the author seems to have begun it with some fire; the characters of Pandarus and Thersites are promising enough; but, as if he grew weary of his task after an entrance or two, he lets them fall; and the latter part of the tragedy is nothing but a confusion of drums and trumpets, excursions, and alarms. The chief persons, who give name to the tragedy, are left alive; Cressida is false and is not punished. Yet, after all, because the play was Shakespeare's and that there appeared in some places of it the admirable genius of the author, I undertook to remove that heap of rubbish under which many excellent thoughts lay wholly buried. Accordingly I new-modeled the plot, threw out many unnecessary persons, improved those characters which were begun and left unfinished, as Hector, Troilus, Pandarus, and Thersites, and added that of Andromache. After this I made, with no small trouble, an order and connection of all the scenes; removing them from the places where they were inartificially set; and, though it was impossible to keep them all unbroken, because the scene must be sometimes in the city and sometimes in the camp, yet I have so ordered them, that there is a coherence of them with one another, and a dependence on the main design; no leaping from Troy to the Grecian tents, and thence back again in the same act, but a due proportion of time allowed for every motion.

"I need not say that I have refined his language, which before was obsolete; but I am willing to acknowledge that as I have often drawn his English nearer to our times, so I have sometimes conformed my own to his; and, consequently, the language is not altogether so pure as it is significant.

"The scenes of Pandarus and Cressida, of Troilus and Pandarus, of Andromache with Hector and the Trojans, in the second act, are wholly new; together with that of Nestor and Ulysses with Thersites, and that of Thersites with Ajax and Achilles. I will not weary my reader with the scenes which are added of Pandarus and the lovers, in the third, and those of Thersites, which are wholly altered; but I cannot omit the last scene in it, which is almost half the act, betwixt Troilus and Hector. . . . The beginning scenes of the fourth act are either added or changed wholly by me; the middle of it is Shakespeare altered and mingled with my own; three or four of the last scenes are altogether new. And the whole fifth act, both the plot and the writing are my own additions."

This is followed by what is perhaps Dryden's most ambitious piece of dramatic criticism, "The Grounds of Criticism in Tragedy," to the principles set forth in which he endeavored to make Shakespeare's play, by alteration, conform.

Dryden's having been at pains to indicate his chief modifications will allow the forgoing of an extended description of his play and the confining of our account of it to an exhibition of the manner in which the amalgamation of his own additions with the original is made and to the giving of the details of some of the changes he either merely mentions or does not note in the preface. The "unnecessary persons" omitted are Cassandra, Helen, Paris, Deiphobus, Helenus, and Antenor. Shakespeare's prologue is superseded by one put into the mouth of the ghost of Shakespeare.

Act First is virtually as in the original, with the exception of considerable abridgment and a rearrangement of scenes.

The Second Act is a heterogeneous mixture of Shakespeare and Dryden. The first scene is a part of Shakespeare's II, 2, joined with a new part consisting of a dialogue between Hector and Andromache, in which she exhorts him to challenge some warrior of the Greeks. The second scene, which is between Pandarus and Cressida and Pandarus and Troilus, is mostly new, there being about twenty lines only from Shakespeare's III, 2. The third scene, in which Nestor, Ulysses, Thersites, and Ajax appear, is made up of parts of I, 3, and II, 2, of the original, and of much additional matter.

The Third Act is altered slightly, various parts of Shakespeare's corresponding act being united with new material, until the concluding scene between Hector and Troilus, which is entirely new. This last feature, the preface states, was suggested by Betterton. It is an imitation of a quarrel between Agamemnon and Menelaus in the "Iphigenia in Aulis" of Euripedes, and Dryden was particularly proud of it. We prefer, however, the fine scene between Achilles and Ulysses, which, save a few lines put in Dryden's IV, 2, is rejected to make room for it.

In the Fourth Act is initiated the principal change in the play, that in the character of Cressida. Shakespeare, following Chaucer, represents her as false to Troilus, but Dryden, to please the ladies, makes her faithful, thus going counter to the hitherto invariable portrayal of her. In Dryden, Calchas advises her to dissemble love to Diomede, which she does, giving him — to mention an unnecessary change in an unimportant particular — a ring, instead of a sleeve as in Shakespeare. Among several minor changes, Troilus is made to fight with Diomede. Lines are borrowed from several scenes of the original, but the greater part of the act is the reviser's own.

It follows, of course, that the Fifth Act is practically a new one, although parts of several of Shakespeare's scenes are used. Cressida, on being reproached by Troilus, stabs herself to prove her innocence and dies forgiving Troilus, who bitterly curses himself for believing her false. Troilus then kills Diomede and is in turn killed by Achilles, and the Greeks are victorious.

All will agree with Scott that "the modern improvements of Dryden show to very little advantage beside the venerable structure to which they have been attached." The adaptation to the central plot theory is made with some skill, but the carrying out of this caused Dryden to omit some of the best passages in the play, such as, for example, the fine speech of Ulysses to Achilles on time's so quickly causing one's deeds and oneself to be forgotten. The change in the conception of Cressida would not have been accepted in Shakespeare's time when her infidelity was proverbial, and her reputed punishment of becoming a beggar and leper was a matter of literary allusion. But by Dryden's time her story and the prejudice against her had doubtless been largely forgotten, or, if remembered, did not stand in the way of transforming her when the canons of so-called dramatic art demanded such a change. The rule which is responsible for this new characterization of the heroine of this play has been sufficiently noticed and criticised in the general discussion and so this feature need not be treated further here. This is not the only rule of the kind, however, applied by Dryden in revising the play, for poetical justice is also conspicuous, Troilus, who is left alive by Shakespeare, being killed in punishment for his doubt of Cressida's fidelity, and, what is a strange variation from classical story for so good a classical scholar as Dryden to make, Diomede being slain by Troilus for his attempt to alienate Cressida's affections.

There is no gainsaying that, for the stage, parts of Shakespeare's play need rearrangement, and this Dryden has in some respects done satisfactorily, but he and his times are strongly to be censured for his not resting content with such treatment. The dénouement as it is in Shakespeare and Chaucer is much more true to life and therefore artistic than it is in Dryden, where there is a resort to the conventional expedient of the heroine's stabbing herself to establish her innocence.

The additions which Dryden makes show considerable invention, but are unnecessary and take the place of superior parts of the original. Among other minor departures from Shakespeare, he has enlarged the parts of Pandarus and Thersites and put into their mouths language which descends to ribaldry, a feature that is a wretched substitute for the several characters whose omission has been noted and their speeches.

Dryden's opinion of Shakespeare's language and style has been already given, so then we are not surprised to find that throughout the play he has subjected the diction to the process of refining, as he called it, and has rendered it such as the putting into practice of his ideas on this point would lead us to expect it to be. An example of the result of this treatment will be more effective, if compared with the corresponding passage in Shakespeare, in showing the extent of the transformation than any amount of description. I have chosen a part of Nestor's reply to Agamemnon in I, 3:

> " With due observance of thy sovereign seat,
> Great Agamemnon, Nestor shall apply
> Thy well-weighed words. In struggling with misfortune
> Lies the true proof of virtue. On smooth seas
> How many bauble-boats dare set their sails
> And make an equal way with firmer vessels!
> But let the tempest once enrage that sea,
> And then behold the strong-ribbed argosy,
> Bounding between the ocean and the air,
> Like Perseus mounted on his Pegasus,
> Then where are those weak rivals of the main?
> Or, to avoid the tempest, fled to port,
> Or made a prey to Neptune. Even thus
> Do empty show, and true prized worth divide
> In storms of fortune."

What an emasculation has here been effected! In view of his violence both to plot and to diction we shall again have to find "Glorious John" guilty of dramatic felony, the only mitigating circumstance which inclines us to mercy being the fact of his living in the times when he did, which relieves him largely of the responsibility for his literary notions and actions.

CHAPTER VII. CORIOLANUS — TITUS ANDRONICUS — ROMEO AND JULIET — TIMON OF ATHENS

Coriolanus

THIS tragedy has been several times altered. The first remodeling was made by Tate in 1682, and the spirit in which it was done will be seen from the reviser's remarks in his epistle dedicatory: "Much of what is offered here, is fruit that grew in the richness of his [Shakespeare's] soil; and, whatever the superstructure prove, it was my good fortune to build upon a rock. Upon a close view of this story, there appeared in some passages no small resemblance with the busy faction of our time. And I confess, I chose rather to set the parallel nearer to sight than to throw it off at further distance." He says further that the moral of the scenes of his version is loyalty or submission and adherence to established lawful power.

The prologue tells what Tate has done.

> " He only ventures to make gold from ore
> And turn to money, what lay dead before."

He thought it necessary to change the title, so he called his play "The Ingratitude of a Commonwealth, or the Fall of Caius Martius Coriolanus."

Act I, scene 1, aside from some omission and much change of diction, is about as in Shakespeare. Scene

2 is partly like I, 3. The lines before "Enter a gentlewoman" are versified. Valeria is made a "talkative fantastical" lady, her talk being like that of a society woman of Tate's time. Scene 3 is like I, 4, and I, 5, save that Lartius is omitted. Scene 4 is a combination of scenes 8 and 9.

The first scene of Act II is made up of the parts of II, 1 and II, 2 that are in verse, but the language is greatly altered. Scene 2 is like II, 3.

Act III, scene 1, follows the original. Then a new scene is added, which is between Volumnia and Valeria, the latter of whom is passing by in a chair. Valeria talks garrulously of various things, such as Coriolanus's obstinacy, her dress, her lovers, etc. Parts of III, 2, III, 3, and IV, 1, follow.

The Fourth Act is a jumble of portions of Acts IV and V from IV, 4, to V, 3, inclusive. The scenes in Antium are transferred to Corioli. A part of V, 2 which is in prose in Shakespeare, is put in verse. In this act is introduced a new character who is to play a considerable part in the next act, namely, Nigridius, a villain discharged by Coriolanus and received by Aufidius. Up to this point, Tate has not departed widely from Shakespeare, but in the next and last act, he alters so greatly that little of the original remains. The act opens with a scene in which the women of the play are the participants and speakers. Volumnia has heard that Nigridius is plotting against Coriolanus and determines to go to Corioli with Virgilia and young Martius. A scene follows between Aufidius and Nigridius, in which the latter exhorts the former to take revenge on Coriolanus. They learn that the Volscian senate is trying Coriolanus and Aufidius plans to go to the council hall and kill him. The scene then changes to the council hall and is somewhat like Shakespeare's last scene. But Tate, however, piles agony on agony. Coriolanus and Aufidius fight and are both mortally wounded. The former does not die immediately, as in Shakespeare, but is kept alive for some time. Before he dies, Virgilia comes in, also in a dying condition, from a wound which she has herself inflicted to avoid the worse fate of being ravished by Nigridius. At this point, Aufidius dies. Then Nigridius enters and boasts of having broken the bones of young Martius. Volumnia, raving mad, comes in with her grandson and, seizing a sword, kills Nigridius. The boy dies and finally Coriolanus makes a dying speech and the play ends.

Tate's modifications are not wholly bad, for he has made a few judicious, or at least permissible, omissions and transpositions in the first four acts. But far too much is rejected to make room for his own Fifth Act. Besides, he takes great and unwarrantable liberties with the dialogue and adds much that is unnecessary and uninspired. His transmogrification of Valeria into a contemporary fashionable woman is absurd.

When we come to the Fifth Act, in which Tate exercises his own invention so freely, we find much that is contemptible. He wrote the act to point the moral announced in his dedication. Coriolanus comes to grief because he has been disloyal to established authority. He is kept alive to view the misfortunes of the various members of his family as a further punishment for this disloyalty. Aufidius and Nigridius, for the introduction of the latter of whom there is no warrant and no necessity, lose their lives as poetical justice for their plotting against Coriolanus. As has been noted before, Shakespeare had not observed this "rule of art" in the case of the former character and so Tate seized the opportunity to "improve" on him in this respect. On how much higher an artistic plane Shakespeare's treatment of the character of Aufidius is, all will now admit.

The finale as altered is, moreover, a revolting exhibition of physical horrors which nowadays would not be put in a drama, let alone be witnessed with satisfaction by an audience. Altogether, this Fifth Act of Tate's is a wretched graft upon the story and Shakespeare's play, and he merits nothing but censure for his performance.

A second alteration of Coriolanus was made in 1719 by John Dennis, whom we have met before as a critic of Shakespeare's art and as an alterer of his "Merry Wives of Windsor."

Dennis also felt it to be necessary to change the title, which he made, "The Invader of his Country, or the Fatal Resentment." In spite of the facts that a great part of the tragedy is Shakespeare's and that the part of Coriolanus was well acted by Booth, the play was produced only three times and then withdrawn, to the great displeasure of Dennis, the managers of Drury Lane maintaining that it was not sufficiently profitable. For my account of this play I shall have to rely upon Genest.

Dennis's First Act consists of the military scenes only. His Second Act begins with a scene between Volumnia and Virgilia. The part of Shakespeare's scene 1 between Menenius and the tribunes and Menenius and Volumnia and the scene in the Capitol are omitted, as well as some other and minor portions. A good deal of low comedy is added to the parts of the citizens in scene 3 of the original. In Act III, he badly mutilates the first scene, especially the part between Coriolanus and the tribunes. The act ends with a tasteless scene in which Coriolanus takes leave of Virgilia, the dialogue being out of keeping with the characters. The chief additions to the Fourth Act, which begins at about Shakespeare's IV, 4, are more low comedy speeches and a conclusion to the scene at Rome, in which the citizens are represented as carrying off the tribunes with the intention of hurling them down from the Tarpeian Rock. In Act V, the scenes of the original in which Menenius appears are excised. Aufidius and his officers begin the act; soon Coriolanus enters and then Volumnia and the other women. Volumnia draws a dagger and threatens, but does not actually attempt, to stab herself. When the women have gone out, Coriolanus fights with Aufidius and kills him. The Volscians then mortally wound Coriolanus, who does not die, however, until after his mother and wife reënter. The play is concluded by a speech made by Cominius.

Fully half the play is Dennis's and the Shakespearean portion is altered for the worse, so that the whole is a bad mangling of the tragedy. The change in the conclusion in the case of Aufidius is, as with Tate, to satisfy poetical justice by having him die. The tribunes Sicinius and Brutus are also killed off for the same reason. Again we see what havoc the application of an artificial notion can work with a play of Shakespeare's. Dennis has but stultified himself by attempting to improve Shakespeare, the absence of the superior enlightenment and knowledge of dramatic art he believed himself to possess being amply demonstrated by his performance in this instance, as it had been also in the case of his revision of "The Merry Wives of Windsor."

The poet James Thomson in 1747 finished a

tragedy of "Coriolanus," which is entirely independent of Shakespeare's play, a different source having been followed. His play, which was not acted and printed until 1749, the year after his death, is written in a cold classical manner and, indeed, is one of those tragedies in which, to use Doctor Johnson's phrase, "Declamation roared, whilst Passion slept." It would not be mentioned here but for its effect on later alterations of Shakespeare's play.

On December 10, 1754, was acted at Covent Garden, a version of "Coriolanus" made by amalgamating Shakespeare with Thomson. It had previously been performed at Dublin and it is probable that it was compiled by the elder Sheridan, though it was published anonymously. A subtitle, "The Roman Matron," was added. An examination of the play proves it to be rather a version of Thomson with additions from Shakespeare than an alteration of the latter's drama. It may be of interest to see how the combination of the two plays has been effected.

The First Act of Shakespeare's play is omitted, with the exception of the scene between Coriolanus's mother and wife, to whom the compiler gives the names he found in Thomson, who, following his sources, made the mother Veturia and the wife Volumnia. The First Act of the new play is this scene and Shakespeare's Second Act. Act II is Shakespeare's Third Act with some of Coriolanus's most effective speeches discarded, as in Dennis. Act III consists of Thomson's First Act with additions from his Second Act. Act IV is all Thomson, except the second scene which is composed of parts of three scenes from Shakespeare with additional lines about hurling the tribunes from the Tarpeian Rock (again an indebtedness to Dennis). The Fifth Act is, save about twenty lines from Shakespeare, Thomson's.

If the play be regarded as an alteration of Shakespeare it is a very bad one, for many fine scenes have been omitted to make room for dull ones from Thomson. Compiling a play from two authors is an execrable practice and unfair to both, as justice can be done to neither. In this case, the jumbling of two plays so entirely different in style and conception has produced a very curious piece of patchwork.

Again, J. P. Kemble, whose great part was Coriolanus, made an alteration, which was acted at Drury Lane in 1789. What might have been a legitimate and judicious abridgment and adaptation of Shakespeare's play is spoiled by borrowing from Thomson in the Fourth and Fifth Acts. In the Fourth Act especially, there is certainly no necessity for a resort to such a practice, as Shakespeare has provided an abundance of material. As it is, five whole scenes are rejected in favor of inferior matter from Thomson. In the Fifth Act, the action and dialogue are more Thomson's than Shakespeare's. The latter's conclusion being a little lame, Kemble saw fit to attempt to improve it by introducing the quarrel scene between Coriolanus and Aufidius from Thomson. Granting that he has accomplished his object, one cannot but wish that he had not known Thomson's play, or, instead of resorting to it had confined himself to Shakespeare. The same judiciousness he had exhibited in revising the first three acts would probably, if applied in treating the last two, have produced a definitive acting version of Shakespeare's play.

OF SHAKESPEARE 127

Titus Andronicus

An alteration of this partly Shakespearean tragedy of blood was given at the Theatre Royal in 1678. It was by the dramatist Edward Ravenscroft, who published it nine years later.

As to plot, Ravenscroft's revision does not differ in important respects from the original. A good deal, however, is omitted, and there are some transpositions, not in every case bad, and also considerable additions. These last, which mainly take the direction of adding to the gruesomeness of a play already nauseously bloody, are interesting as showing that the representation of physical horrors to an extent which would not be tolerated by an audience of our day, was apparently pleasurable to the playgoers of the Restoration period. Indeed, Ravenscroft tells us that his play was successful.

To what extremes in this respect the alterer went, will appear when we learn that every dish served up to the Emperor and Tamora contains parts of the hearts and tongues of the Queen's sons and their blood is mingled with all the wine drunk; that Tamora stabs her child by the Moor; that the latter, in a burst of admiration for his paramour's transcendent act of iniquity and in emulation of her fiendishness, offers to eat the dead child; and finally that this most detestable of villains is tortured on the rack and burned to death before the audience.

Ravenscroft himself boasts of his "improvements." "Compare the old play with this," he says, with no little exaggeration, in his preface, "you'll find that none in all that author's works ever received greater alterations and additions, the language not only refined, but many scenes entirely new, besides most of the principal characters heightened, and the plot much increased." Lost in wonder that scenes of such horror, which are revolting even to read about, could be thus spoken of, we feel that we can say nothing further than that we dissent most heartily from any such favorable opinion of this alteration as that of its not too modest maker.

Romeo and Juliet

This "Song of Songs of Romantic Passion" (Gollancz) was subjected in the period of which we are treating to a varied fate. It had been revived as early as March, 1662, and was one of the first plays to be modified. Downes says: "This play was, after some time, altered by James Howard so as to preserve Romeo and Juliet alive and to end happily. It was played alternately as a tragedy one day and as a tragi-comedy another, for several times together." What further changes, besides that of the catastrophe, were made is not known. The playbill gives as one of the characters Count Paris's wife, who must have been introduced in some way in the play as altered.

Here we have probably the first application to Shakespeare of the principle of poetical justice, the lack of truth of which to nature and experience is so evident to anyone not blinded by preconceived false theories of art. This mistaken notion and its pernicious effect on Shakespeare's plays have already been discussed. In this case, much as human nature impels us to wish for the happiness of the lovers, we are aware that, as is so often the case in real life, such violence of passion cannot but have a tragic outcome, and, further, that their lives are a necessary sacrifice to bring about the end of the deadly civil feud in which they are so hopelessly involved.

Otway's "Caius Marius," (1680), which is, strictly, not a version of Shakespeare at all, but a borrowing, or rather a theft, from him, certainly bears a highly curious relation to "Romeo and Juliet," from which it is in part taken.

That Otway, who, at his best, could produce the finest tragedies of his age, should stoop to commit such a literary crime as this play exhibits — he says himself that he has "rifled him [Shakespeare] of half a play" — can be explained only as due to the exigency of his pecuniary affairs. The quarrel between Marius and Sulla doubtless occurred to him as a suitable subject for a tragedy, and, having, as usual, to write for bread, he was probably anxious to have his play ready at the earliest possible moment. The feud between the houses of Montague and Capulet being familiar to him, he evidently, in an evil moment, conceived the idea of transferring its incidents to the enmity between the partisans of Marius and those of Sulla, and of making use also of as much of Shakespeare's dialogue as his plan permitted. "To such low shifts, of late," says he, by way of apology, "are poets worn."

In treating of this strange hodgepodge of Shakespeare and Roman history, I shall pay attention only to the Shakespearean portions, as being those that come within the scope of my subject. As to the character of the parts of the play which are Otway's own, no more need be said than that they follow fairly closely the historical facts.

Caius Marius is represented as having a son, Marius Junior, who is in love with Lavinia, daughter of Metellus. The last is a partisan of Sulla and wishes his chief to be his son-in-law. This situation affords opportunity to introduce several scenes and many passages from "Romeo and Juliet." The greater part of the Nurse's character is retained and Sulpitius uses some of Mercutio's speeches.

The First Act is almost all Otway's. A mangled form of the description of Queen Mab is spoken by Sulpitius. In the Second Act, Metellus expresses to Lavinia his desire that she should be married, as Lady Capulet does to Juliet; most of the Nurse's lines appear, but in prose; and Metellus speaks some of Capulet's lines in III, 5, of "Romeo and Juliet." Sulpitius conjures for Marius Junior, as Mercutio for Romeo in Shakespeare, and then follows the garden scene between Marius Junior and Lavinia, most of the lines being taken from Shakespeare. The Third Act includes considerable of "Romeo and Juliet." Lavinia's nurse comes to young Marius and is quizzed by Sulpitius. Lavinia speaks Juliet's soliloquy in III, 2, and then comes a scene between her and the Nurse somewhat as in Shakespeare's II, 5. In the Fourth Act, about twenty lines of Shakespeare's III, 5, are introduced in the parting scene between Marius Junior and Lavinia; the Priest of Hymen gives her a sleeping potion; she speaks some lines from IV, 1; and, after the priest goes out, Juliet's soliloquy in IV, 3. Shakespeare is again laid under a heavy contribution in Otway's last act. The Nurse discovers Lavinia apparently dead, Marius Junior hears of her death, soliloquizes as in Shakespeare, and buys poison of an apothecary. At the tomb young Marius kills the priest, not knowing who he is, and drinks the poison, but before he dies Lavinia awakes. She later kills herself, and the play ends with some lines, partly Mercutio's, spoken by Sulpitius.

From this brief account of the relation of Otway's play to Shakespeare's, it will be seen that Otway speaks truly when he declares he has pilfered half a play. He makes some changes, in the way of abridgment, in the passages he steals, and to some of the scenes he follows he adds considerable of his own.

It is not worth while to waste any time or words upon such a contemptible piece of thieving as this. It would seem as if Otway might have found material enough for a play without resorting to such an expedient. The only redeeming feature of it all is that he had sufficient good sense not to alter greatly what he stole, but this scarcely makes his sin the less. His main change, the restoration of Lavinia to consciousness before Marius Junior dies, is pronounced by Genest to be an improvement, and this device is retained, to anticipate a little, in Theophilus Cibber's version and in Garrick's and the revision of the latter by Kemble. Whether it heightens the pathos of the situation or not is a debatable question. It may make it a little more tragic, but it seems almost too much piling on of agony to have Romeo discover that he has poisoned himself unnecessarily.

Theophilus Cibber's version of "Romeo and Juliet" was performed at the Haymarket Theatre in 1744. The chief departure from the original is in the borrowing of ideas, lines, and passages from Otway's "Caius Marius," an action which is not altogether surprising as that tragedy had been frequently acted.

In the First Act, Cibber follows Shakespeare fairly closely, but a few hints and lines are borrowed from Otway and there is no mention of Rosaline. Act II has about eight lines from Otway. The description of Queen Mab is put in this act. In the

Third Act, which is not materially altered, about nine lines are taken from Valentine's soliloquy, when he is banished by the Duke, in "Two Gentlemen of Verona." There are no changes of importance in the Fourth Act. Some scenes are abridged, between twenty and thirty lines are introduced from Otway, and a little of Cibber's own composition is added to Juliet's first soliloquy. In Act V, Cibber follows Otway in making Juliet wake before Romeo dies, and is indebted to his predecessor for considerable of the dialogue.

Cibber deserves credit for having drawn the attention of playgoers to a tragedy of Shakespeare's that had not been acted for eighty years, and a negative sort of merit is his for refraining, to the extent that he does, from tampering with the plot. But this is overbalanced to his discredit by his adulteration of Shakespeare's gold with the base metal of Otway, by which process he has put himself in the number of that contemptible herd of literary cobblers who have stultified themselves by destroying in this way the organism of an author. We have the right to demand of a reviser that, at least, he give us Shakespeare and not Shakespeare mingled with the dross of his inferiors.

Garrick's version, later slightly revised by Kemble, was first acted at Drury Lane, November 29, 1748. This adaptation does Garrick no credit, but rather considerable discredit. Among the many minor changes may be mentioned that of the age of Juliet from fourteen to eighteen, the removal in many cases of the rime, and the addition of a line or two from Congreve's "Mourning Bride." As in Cibber, there is no reference to Rosaline, Romeo being represented at first as having already seen Juliet. This

necessitates considerable alteration and is a bad
change, as it removes one of the causes of Romeo's
misfortunes, his desertion of his earlier love. The
fifth scene of Act III, with its beautiful poetry, is, to
our amazement, discarded. The first scene of Act
V is the funeral of Juliet, consisting of a dirge (air
and chorus) with no dialogue, and is an unnecessary,
unwelcome, and rather contemptible addition. In
the last scene, Juliet wakes, as in Otway and Cibber,
before Romeo dies.

From the preface to Charles Marsh's "Cymbeline" as republished in 1762, it appears that he also revised "Romeo and Juliet." The elder Sheridan is said to have made an alteration for representation at Dublin, and John Lee one for the Edinburgh theatre. Nothing further, however, is known of any of these three.

Timon of Athens

The literary fortunes of this play after the Restoration were varied, for it was several times altered, the changes being in the direction of a complication of the plot through the addition of feminine characters. The first was made in 1678 by Thomas Shadwell, the Mac Flecknoe and Og of Dryden's satire, whom we have met before as the maker of "The Tempest" into an opera. Shadwell's version had a dedication to the Duke of Buckingham, in the course of which he says: "It has the inimitable hand of Shakespeare in it, which never made more masterly strokes than in this. Yet I can truly say, I have made it into a play." The prologue contains the same modest declaration. We shall learn, therefore, from a description of this version what was that indispensable requisite for a play which Shakespeare had failed to provide.

There are a number of changes and additions in the dramatis personæ. The lords are given Greek names; Flavius is called Demetrius, and Lucilius, Diphilus; Ventidius is omitted, but is mentioned in the play as Lampridius; a musician is added to the number of those living on the liberality of Timon; and — here we get a hint of the nature of the process of making Shakespeare's "Timon" a play — there are introduced Evandra, a mistress whom Timon has abandoned, but who is faithful to him to the end, and Melissa, a woman whom he is about to marry, but who deserts him in adversity. The part of Apemantus is enlarged as is also that of Timon's steward.

The First Act opens with a scene, at first between Demetrius and the poet, but soon with the musician and others participating. In this there are only a few lines from Shakespeare. After Timon enters, a good deal of the original is used, but Apemantus has much more to say (his speeches are put in verse) and Nicias, father of Melissa, is introduced, he and Timon conversing about the latter's approaching marriage with Melissa. The last scene is a long one between Timon and Evandra. She beseeches him not to marry Melissa, but to be constant to her, telling him that marriage is a slavery from which nothing but death can free him — the opinion of that institution current in court circles in the time of Shadwell. Timon professes regard for her, but declares he cannot live without Melissa.

The first scene of Act II is a dressing-room scene, Melissa being in process of adornment by her maid Chloe for attendance at Timon's masque. Then follows a love scene between her and Timon, at the end

of which they depart for the feast. The scene then
changes to Timon's house, where at first Apemantus
and the poet are talking. After a while the senators
enter and finally Timon and his lady love. Apemantus again says much more, most of it in verse, than in
Shakespeare. The banquet comes next, after which
a masque of Shadwell's composition is enacted before the guests. Evandra, Chloe, who brings Melissa a letter from Alcibiades, and other women enter
masked and witness the entertainment. At the conclusion of the masque all leave except Timon and
Evandra. She tells Timon she cannot live without
him and offers to stab herself. Timon orders Diphilus to take her home and promises to come to her.
Demetrius comes in to tell Timon of the loss of his
wealth, but the latter refuses to listen to anything
about business.

The Third Act opens with Demetrius's informing
Timon of his bankruptcy as in Shakespeare's II, 2,
and with the dispatching of the servants to the several lords. Then follows a scene in which Apemantus in the porch of the Stoics is speaking to the Senators and people, not Stoic but Cynic doctrine, as he
rails at everything. Timon's servants enter and are
turned off by those to whom they had been sent. In
the next scene, Melissa tells Chloe not to admit anyone from Timon. Alcibiades comes in in disguise,
pulls off his mask, and a love scene ensues between
Melissa and him. Then Timon is attacked by his
creditors, slighted by his former friends, and even
by his servant Diphilus and Melissa, who passes by.
Evandra, however, consoles him. The next scene is
the false banquet, but, in Shadwell, toads and snakes
are substituted for the warm water of the original.

The Fourth Act begins as in Shakespeare with

Timon's soliloquy, but Shadwell has somewhat altered it. The fifth scene of Act III (Alcibiades and the Senate), also with alterations, comes next. The succeeding scene opens with Timon's soliloquy in IV, 3 (of course altered and for the worse). Evandra then appears and is at first repulsed by Timon who finally, however, receives her and shows her his new-found wealth. On Apemantus's approach she retires to the cave. The scene between that worthy and Timon is somewhat abridged. The parts of the thieves and of Flavius (Demetrius), who in Shadwell has deserted Timon, are discarded. A part of V, 1, then follows, the poet and painter entering to Timon. Melissa, who has heard that Timon has found an abundance of gold, comes and seeks reconcilement, but he rejects her and professes his attachment to Evandra.

In Act V, Timon and Evandra have the first scene. He speaks of his death and she declares she will not survive him. The scene with the Senators, altered from V, 1, ensues. The next scene is that between Alcibiades and the courtesans, Shakespeare's IV, 3. Then the Senators surrender to Alcibiades (Shakespeare's V, 4, much altered). Timon dies in the next scene and Evandra stabs herself. Melissa is rejected by Alcibiades, and Apemantus is dragged in. He rails at Alcibiades, but is spared by the great soldier because he is a friend of Socrates. The play closes with an harangue by Alcibiades to the Senators, who enter with halters on their necks, and a lament over the death of Timon.

Now, we know what is necessary to constitute a play, namely, the treatment of the passion of love. The development of the story of Timon's change from prodigality to misanthropy was not, in the view of the critics and dramatists of Shadwell's day, a sufficient motif for a play. To their Frenchified taste there must be love intrigue or there was no play. Shakespeare's play had practically no female characters and hence fell far short of being a real drama. This thrusting of amorous intrigues into Shakespeare's plays was, as we have seen, one of the leading principles of alteration, affecting especially the histories. As I have already sufficiently discussed the nature of this principle and the effect of its application to Shakespeare's plays, nothing further in this direction is called for here. That it did not improve this play is self-evident.

The many minor additions and changes that Shadwell made are in general for the worse. The character of Apemantus has not been heightened by the extensive additions to it, and the part of Flavius (Shadwell's Demetrius) has been spoiled by making him faithless. The scenes in which the women appear, as independent matter, are not wholly without power, for Shadwell was a better dramatist than Dryden's scurrilous satire would lead us to think. As a revision of Shakespeare, however, this play is a failure, but one may say in its favor that it is not so bad as some manufactured by greater names.

In 1768 was published "Timon of Athens" as altered from Shakespeare and Shadwell by James Love (whose real name was Dance), an actor and author of no high degree of merit. Love's version had been acted at Richmond. The following is an account of the play, condensed from Genest.

Act I differs but little from Shakespeare; a song from Shadwell is introduced in the banquet scene. Act II is mostly from Shakespeare, but the scene in which Timon is dunned is omitted, and one between

Timon and Evandra, from Shadwell, is substituted. Shadwell's Melissa is omitted, but a good deal is said about her. The first two scenes of Shakespeare's Third Act are put in this act. The course of Act III is as follows: first come Shakespeare's III, 3, and III, 4; then another scene between Timon and Evandra from Shadwell; and finally the Senate scene and banquet of warm water. Act IV differs but little from Shakespeare, except that Evandra appears and speaks some of the lines given to Flavius in Shakespeare. Some dialogue from Shadwell is also used. The first part of the Fifth Act follows Shakespeare. It begins with a soliloquy by Timon, transposed from the scene between him and Apemantus. The thieves and Flavius are omitted, and then all, with the exception of a few lines, is Shakespeare, until after Alcibiades has appeared before the walls. The scene between Timon and Evandra from Shadwell comes next, their deaths, however, not taking place on the stage. The play concludes with a short scene between Alcibiades and the Senators, which is partly from Shakespeare and partly from Shadwell.

There is nothing here to call for extended comment. Some little credit is due Love for not modifying what he took from Shakespeare, for rather improving Shadwell's part of the play, and for refraining almost entirely from adding anything of his own. His play is better than Shadwell's version, and Cumberland's, next to be considered, and it is to be regretted that the compiler did not have the good sense to confine himself to Shakespeare.

At Drury Lane, December 4, 1771, "Timon of Athens" was revived with alterations by Richard Cumberland, author of nearly fifty dramas, of which "The West Indian" is the best known, of some interesting memoirs, and of many miscellaneous works.

Cumberland makes a number of marked changes, the first of which is the furnishing of Timon with a daughter, Evanthe, to whom Alcibiades and Lucius make love. This is a very bad addition, for, as Davies observes, Timon's throwing away on sycophants that wealth which should have been his child's portion extinguishes all pity for him. This introduction of a daughter to Timon causes most of the changes Cumberland has made in the first four acts. Although he sometimes wisely abridges, he has discarded much of the best of the original to make room for scenes in which she takes part. Lucius's love for Evanthe cools when he finds Timon's money is gone, but Alcibiades does not desert her.

When he came to the Fifth Act, Cumberland chose to rewrite it almost entirely. The Senators appear on the walls and surrender the city to Alcibiades, who promises to spare all but his own and Timon's enemies. Evanthe intercedes for the citizens. In the next scene, it comes to light that the treasure which Timon has found had been hidden by Lucullus — an instance of the operation of poetical justice. Alcibiades' soldiers pillage Lucius's house, — poetical justice again. The scene then changes to a wild country. Timon, supported by Flavius, is met by Evanthe and Alcibiades, who request him to return to Athens. Thereupon Timon throws aside his misanthropy, is kind to his daughter, and gives her to Alcibiades. The play ends with Timon's death.

Cumberland, by making this decided change in the characterization of Timon, has largely removed the lesson of Shakespeare's play, the purpose of which is to show the punishment which results from lack of self-restraint, and in general to condemn misanthropy. The debasement of Timon effected by giving such a prodigal a daughter and thus making his fault worse, has already been indicated. Like Shadwell, Cumberland has elevated the character of Alcibiades by omitting the courtesans and by making him a model man and lover, with a loss thereby of historical truth. In one respect his alteration is better than Shadwell's, namely, in that he makes little modification in those scenes of the original which he retains, whereas his predecessor left very few lines into which something of his own was not thrust. His great fault is identical with Shadwell's, and all other would-be improvers; he has discarded too much of Shakespeare to put in too much material of his own composition, which coalesces badly with the original. In his "advertisement" he expresses the wish that he could have brought the play upon the stage with less violence to its author. Had his desire been sincere there is no reason why he might not have achieved it without any very great difficulty. Apparently, he was unable to resist the temptation to borrow from the earlier reviser, which his imbuement with similar dramatic notions doubtless made alluring to him. He must be reckoned then a particeps criminis of the other.

Again, in 1786, an alteration of "Timon" with additions from Shadwell was brought out. This time the compiler was Hull, the friend of Shenstone, whom we have met before as an adapter of "The Comedy of Errors." I have not seen a copy of this. From the list of characters it appears that Evandra and Melissa were borrowed from Shadwell.

The revision of Timon which was acted at Drury Lane in 1816, although a few lines from Cumberland are introduced in the last scene, is practically only a stage version made by omitting portions, usually with propriety. The adapter in this case was the Hon. George Lamb, who was one of the early contributors to the *Edinburgh Review* and as such was satirized by Byron (as he afterwards owned, unjustly) in "English Bards and Scotch Reviewers." Lamb's chief literary work is a translation of Catullus, which was savagely attacked in "Blackwood's" by "Christopher North."

CHAPTER VIII. JULIUS CÆSAR — MACBETH — HAMLET — KING LEAR — OTHELLO

Julius Cæsar

A REVISION of this play was printed in 1719 as it was purported to have been altered by D'Avenant and Dryden. There is the following note on this in Genest under "Covent Garden, January 31, 1766:" "It being generally known that D'Avenant and Dryden had joined in mangling Shakespeare's 'Tempest,' some person seems to have attributed the alteration of 'Julius Cæsar' to them for that reason, and that alone. It is, however, morally certain that D'Avenant never assisted in altering 'Julius Cæsar,' that being one of the plays assigned to Killigrew and which consequently D'Avenant could not act at his own theatre."

I have not found a copy of this and, as Genest gives no account of it, probably the alterations were slight, it being apparently only the theatre book with changes for the stage. The author of the life of D'Avenant in the "Dictionary of National Biography," stigmatizes it as "wretched," which epithet seems unwarrantably strong, if the above conclusion as to its nature is correct.

There is no better example of the fatuity of attempting to circumscribe the romantic drama by the artificial rules of the classical drama, than the revision now to be considered, the two tragedies which Sheffield made out of this play.

John Sheffield, Earl of Mulgrave, Marquis of

Normandy, and Duke of Buckinghamshire, was a man and writer of no little reputation in his day. He was an intimate friend of, and even a co-worker with, Dryden, who spoke of him as

> "Sharp-judging Adriel, the Muses' friend,
>   Himself a muse,"

and who dedicated to him his "Auranzebe" and his translation of the Æneid. He was also a friend of Pope, who "at the command of His Grace" wrote two of the choruses in the Duke's second play. Of course, living in the age that he did, he would be likely to be a thoroughgoing classicist, and those who have read his verse "Essay on Poetry" will not need to be told that he was in accord with his time. This being the case, one can readily anticipate that, when he set to work to alter "Julius Cæsar," he would have the intention of making it "regular" if possible, and such we find to be the spirit in which his revision was made.

His alterations were never acted, but were published by his duchess in 1722, after his death. In order to observe the unities and to bring Shakespeare's play into harmony with the classical form, he divided it, as has been said, into two plays, which he called "The Tragedy of Julius Cæsar" and "The Death of Marcus Brutus," and furnished each with a prologue and choruses. In the prologue to the first play, he says:

> "Hope to mend Shakespeare! or to match his style!
> 'Tis such a jest would make a stoic smile.
> Too fond of fame, our poet soars too high;
> Yet freely owns he wants the wings to fly;
> That he confesses while he does the fault."

If such was his real opinion we wonder at his vanity in undertaking this well-nigh impossible task. Sheffield is so solicitous lest anyone should think he neglects to observe the unity of time, that he is careful to state that the play begins the day before Cæsar's death and ends within an hour after it.

The alterations in the plot of the first play are slight, but the diction is much changed and there is a good deal of Sheffield's own poetry. In the First Act, all the low comedy is omitted and the offering of the crown is made a part of the action. In Act II, the scene between Brutus and Portia is transformed into an insipid love dialogue. Calpurnia is omitted in Act III, the ill omens being reported by the priests. Act IV is without change as to action. Brutus's address is turned into blank verse, and the Fifth Act ends with Antony's address, the opening lines of which are worth quoting as an example of Sheffield's improvement upon Shakespeare:

> " Friends, countrymen, and Romans, hear me gently;
> I come to bury Cæsar, not to praise him.
> Lo here the fatal end of all his glory:
> The evil that men do, lives after them;
> The good is often bury'd in their graves;
> So let it be with Cæsar. Noble Brutus
> Has told you Cæsar was ambitious:
> If he was so, then he was much to blame;
> And he has dearly paid for his offense.
> I come to do my duty to dead Cæsar."

The second tragedy, having but two acts of the original to draw upon, called for much additional material. Accordingly, the Duke introduces several new characters, as Theodotus, a philosopher; Dolabella; Varius, a young Roman bled at Athens; and

Junia, wife of Cassius and sister of Brutus. In reality, an almost entirely new play is manufactured, as the first three acts are entirely Sheffield's, and althouh the substance of the Fourth and Fifth Acts is Shakespeare's, the words are the Duke's. Many variations are made even when the scenes are founded on Shakespeare. For instance, instead of Pindarus unwillingly holding the sword for Cassius to run upon, the servant kills himself, after which his master, encouraged by his example, or reproached by it, stabs himself. This is precisely as in the case of Eros and Antony, in "Antony and Cleopatra," which probably suggested the change here.

The scene lies at Athens in the first three acts and near Philippi in the last two. The Duke apologizes for thus violating the unity of place:

> "Our scene is Athens;
> But here our author besides other faults
> Of ill expressions and of vulgar thoughts
> Commits one crime that needs an act of grace
> And breaks the law of unity of place."

Truly an audacious thing to do! The unity of time, however, we are informed has been preserved, for the play begins the day before the battle of Philippi and ends with that event. Here the Duke's solicitude has made him absurdly inconsistent, for the movements could not be made from Athens to Philippi in the time, nor could Cassius get back in twenty-four hours from Sardis, where Junia says he has gone. Probably His Grace did not look into the geography of his scene, which is unpardonable in so great a stickler for correctness.

This is the only attempt to give a play of Shakespeare's a strictly classical form, and no reader of the

Duke's plays will have any doubt as to the superiority of Shakespeare's treatment. The best excuse for Sheffield's two plays lies in Shakespeare's duality of heroes. But Brutus is the one upon whom Shakespeare meant to fix the greatest attention, and his purpose is to show how Brutus's misfortunes come as the result of his one error in assassinating Cæsar, doing evil that good may come. Shakespeare's reason for not ending his play with the murder of Cæsar appears in the words of Brutus over Cassius's body:

> "O Julius Cæsar, thou art mighty yet!
> Thy spirit walks abroad and turns our swords
> In our own proper entrails."

But the critics, among them the Duke, did not see this in their shortsightedness.

The battle between the classicists and the romanticists over the unities has been fought and the victory lies with the latter, so there is no necessity for a discussion of them here. Suffice it to say that the attempt to make over Shakespeare's play so as to conform to them has resulted in a very bad alteration of it. Besides his violence to the construction of the play, Sheffield has, in addition, so spoiled the verse, as the specimen of his work given abundantly testifies, that we can have nothing but contempt for his misguided efforts.

Macbeth

One of the most interesting and important alterations was that of "Macbeth," which long kept the stage and which, although finally abandoned, contributed not a little to the later acting copies. The play had been acted after the Restoration at the theatre in Lincoln's Inn Fields, pretty much as Shakespeare wrote it. Furness speaks of a 1673 copy of the play different from the D'Avenant version of the next year. It is, for the most part, a reprint of the First Folio "Macbeth," save that the witch scenes are altered, being very similar to the same scenes in the 1674 version but not coming in the same places. This was doubtless the play as it was acted until the D'Avenant version was put on, and, curiously, it is very much like the acting version of the last century.

"Macbeth," like "The Tempest," was, as has been noted before, one of the plays selected to be made into a sort of opera when it became necessary for the Duke's Company to introduce a novelty to offset the better acting of the King's Company. Accordingly, it was brought out at Dorset Garden with machines for the witches, with dancing, and with much singing. It proved to be very successful and in 1674 was published anonymously. Downes expressly attributes it to D'Avenant, and the internal evidence is strong for his authorship. To the play was prefixed an argument taken verbatim from Heylin's "Cosmography."

The play is considerably changed as to plot, etc., as will be seen from the following account of the marked departures from the original. Ross's name appears in the dramatis personæ, but all his lines are given to other characters. The part of Seyton, as will be seen, is curiously enlarged.

The chief changes in the First Act are the introduction of Macduff into this act (he speaks the lines given to Ross in scene 2 and those given to Ross and Angus in scene 3), and that of Lady Macduff into scene 5. This latter innovation is worthy of note. She is represented as visiting Lady Macbeth. That lady, being anxious to read her husband's letter, prevails upon her guest to retire. D'Avenant did not understand that the words of the letter as given by Shakespeare are only a part of the whole letter, so he absurdly says that an earlier letter had brought "some imperfect news" of Macbeth's meeting with the witches and that "this perhaps may give more full intelligence." The scene is thus changed to introduce a weak scene between the ladies as part of a plan to enlarge the characters of Macduff and his wife.

In the Second Act, the porter scene is omitted (the reason for this has been given earlier) and scene 4 is between Lennox and Seyton, who speak the lines given to Ross and "An Old Man" respectively. Then a long scene, entirely new, is added. Lady Macduff, with maid and servant, is on the heath awaiting her lord, who soon comes in to accompany her home. To them enter the witches, who, after singing two songs and dancing, make a triple prophecy to Macduff as they had previously done to Macbeth. Macduff and his wife are again introduced as in conversation after having arrived at home. They are agreed that Macbeth is responsible for Duncan's death and Macduff determines to defend his country against the tyrant's violence. Yet again they appear after the banquet scene, Lady Macduff pleading with her husband not to go to England, but, when news comes of Banquo's death, begging him to fly.

Seyton has the lines given to "Another Lord" in scene 6 of the original. The last scene of this act is entirely new. It is a witch scene, partly D'Avenant's but mostly a part of a scene in Middleton's "Witch" slightly altered.

The witch scene in Act Fourth is amplified by a

second borrowing from Middleton. Lennox takes the place of Ross in scene 2, and Seyton is the messenger who comes in to warn Lady Macduff of the approach of the murderers. Malcolm and Macduff meet at Birnam Wood instead of in England. Then there is a new scene, first between the ubiquitous Seyton and Macbeth and then between the latter and Lady Macbeth, to whom appears the ghost of Duncan, which is not seen by Macbeth. Lennox reports the murder of Macduff's family to Macduff.

In Act V, the Doctor's lines are given to Seyton; scene 2, participated in by Lennox, Donalbain, and Fleance, is new. The latter two are coming to aid Malcolm. Scenes 6 and 7 are run together and somewhat altered. Lennox is killed by Macbeth, instead of young Siward, who does not appear in the play. Many of the best passages are omitted or mutilated and much stuff is added in this act.

The thing which strikes one most in reading this play is that duplication of important scenes and characters which is a characteristic feature of the D'Avenant alterations and which is consequently pretty good evidence as to the authorship of the version before us. This same feature is, as has been pointed out earlier, found in an incipient stage in "The Law against Lovers," D'Avenant's hodgepodge of "Measure for Measure" and "Much Ado," and again, and this time carried to an absurd extreme, in the version of "The Tempest" which was a joint production of D'Avenant and Dryden, the latter of whom, in the preface to the published play, as we have seen, expressly attributes to D'Avenant the idea of duplication.

This is very inartistic, though Dryden evidently had a contrary opinion, for he commends highly the employment of this feature in the revised "Tempest." Such repetitions do not make the characters, as Dryden said, "more commend each other," but rather detract from the effect by dividing the attention which should be given almost entirely to one scene or set of characters. The evident purpose here is to pair off Macduff and his wife against Macbeth and Lady Macbeth. The former couple are made too prominent to be foils to set off the latter; both lose by the change.

If Seyton had to do all that D'Avenant gives him to do, we do not wonder at his deserting to the English.

The additional and enlarged witch scenes are added in the interest of the operatic feature. Operatic scenes are out of place in a tragedy of this kind; it has to do with more serious events than we are likely to connect with music and dancing. But the prevalent opinion in D'Avenant's time was very different, as witness what Pepys has to say under the date of January 7, 1667: "Saw Macbeth [probably in the form published in 1673, but perhaps in this version], which, though I saw it lately, yet appears a most excellent play in all respects, but especially in divertissement though it be a deep tragedy; which is a strange perfection in a tragedy being most proper here and suitable." This appears to have been the general judgment, for the play thus altered was very popular.

These new and varied witch scenes have been retained in the acting copies of later times. Another survival from D'Avenant is the line " Command they make a halt upon the heath " at the opening of the third scene of Act I in the stage versions of the present day.

It is evident that his version was long more current or more accessible than Shakespeare's play. Steele's quotation of lines from this version in apparent preference to those of Shakespeare has been mentioned. The manner in which the diction has been changed is more irritating to a reader than even the changes in the plot. There are not a half dozen consecutive lines that have not been subjected to unnecessary and arbitrary change, all made in the effort to tone down the style, to get rid of the figurative expressions, and to refine the language. A few examples will give a better idea of the effects of the process than any description however extended.

"Hear it not, Duncan," etc., becomes

> "O Duncan, hear it not, for 'tis a bell
> That rings my coronation and thy knell;"

"Sleep that knits up the ravelled sleave of care" is transmuted into "Sleep that locks up the senses from their care"; and "the deep damnation of his taking off" is diluted into "so black a deed." Again, Macbeth's soliloquy is shortened and opens thus:

> "If it were well when done, then it were well
> It were done quickly; if his death might be
> Without the death of nature in myself,
> And killing my own rest, it would suffice.
> But deeds of this complexion still return
> To plague the doer, and destroy his peace.
> Yet let me think; he's here in double trust,"

and so on. Many of the changes are made through gross misunderstanding of Shakespeare's meaning and seem ridiculous to us, but the corruptions of the text may be responsible for some of them. Others are in the nature of more modern equivalents of obsolete words.

On the whole, while one would not go so far as Steevens and say that "almost every original beauty is either awkwardly disguised or arbitrarily omitted," because by far the greater part of the original is retained, yet it must be said that the alteration is a most atrocious one, and it is well that it is forgotten.

The operatic additions of D'Avenant to the witch scenes of "Macbeth" and to "The Tempest," induced one Thomas Duffet, a milliner, to ridicule the former play in 1674 and the latter in 1675. Duffet wrote a farce "The Empress of Morocco" against Settle's "The Emperor of Morocco," and to it appended as an epilogue, "a new fancy, after the old and most surprising way of 'Macbeth,' performed with new and costly machines, etc." It is made up of dances and coarse songs by Hecate and three witches. Again, a man by the name of Harry Rowe performed "Macbeth" as a puppet show at York.

Another absurd representation was that of "Macbeth" as a *ballet d'action* at the Royal Circus, Saint George's Field, London. "Macbeth" was thus metamorphosed by a Mr. J. C. Cross, to give, it is said, an actor named Elliston, who could not, because attached to a minor theatre, act in the higher characters of the drama, a chance to exhibit his talents in that direction. The full title of this monstrosity is "The History, Murders, Life, and Death of Macbeth." The music and the witches were retained with several portions of the text for Macbeth to speak. There are several new scenes introduced, one being a bedchamber scene in which Duncan is murdered, while asleep, by Macbeth. The same scene is again shown, after the alarm has been given; all the principal characters come on; Macbeth stabs the "sleepy grooms"; and a "picture of horror and surprise" is formed to end the first act.

Such things as this and the Shakespeare travesties are a disgrace to the stage. They serve to show that any real reverence for Shakespeare is of comparatively late origin.

John Lee made a version of "Macbeth," which was played at Edinburgh in 1753. The editors of the "Biographia Dramatica" thus characterize it: "Language is not strong enough to express our contempt of Mr. Lee's performance. If sense, spirit, and versification were ever discoverable in Shakespeare's play, so sure has our reformer laid them all in ruins." I did not learn anything as to the details of this revision.

Hamlet, Prince of Denmark

Garrick in 1772 was so foolish as to make an alteration of Hamlet, thereby demonstrating that his professed reverence for Shakespeare was rather hypocritical and that a good actor may be a very poor playwright. Garrick's revision, which he did not venture to print, although he at first intended to do so, seems to have been undertaken chiefly to free the play from features criticised by Voltaire, who in the preface to his "Semiramis" had called "Hamlet" "a coarse and barbarous piece," and had gone on to point out some of the gross absurdities, with which, in his opinion, the play abounded. According to Davies, Garrick divided the acts differently, but made no great changes in the action or dialogue until toward the end of the play. The plotting scenes between the King and Laertes to destroy Hamlet were entirely changed and Laertes was rendered more es-

154 ALTERATIONS AND ADAPTATIONS

timable. Hamlet, having escaped from Rosencrantz and Guildenstern, returned with a firm resolve to avenge his father's death. The gravediggers and Osric were rejected absolutely; the fate of Ophelia was not mentioned; her funeral was omitted; and the Queen, instead of being poisoned on the stage, was led from her seat and reported to be in an insane condition, due to her sense of guilt. When Hamlet attacked the King, the latter drew his sword, defended himself, and was killed in the rencounter. Laertes and Hamlet then died of mutual wounds.

The account given by Boaden in his "Life of J. P. Kemble," adds a little to this, and differs from it in some respects, especially as to the conclusion. Among the additional particulars, we are told that Garrick cut out the voyage to England and the execution of Rosencrantz and Guildenstern (he must mean the references to Hamlet's artifice to get them killed and to the report of their deserved fate); that all the wisdom of the Prince is omitted; that Hamlet bursts in upon the King and his court and is reproached by Laertes for being the cause of his father's and his sister's deaths; that, when they are both at the height of anger, the King interposes and is stabbed by Hamlet. The remainder of the play is said to have been as follows; "The Queen rushes out, imploring the attendants to save her from her son. Laertes, seeing treason and murder before him, attacks Hamlet to revenge his father, his sister, and his King. He wounds Hamlet mortally, and Horatio is on the point of making Laertes accompany him to the shades, when the Prince commands him to desist, assuring him that it was the hand of Heaven, which administered by Laertes 'That precious balm for all his wounds.'" We then learn that the miserable mother had dropped in a trance before she could reach her chamber door, and Hamlet implores for her " an hour of penitence ere madness end her." He then joins the hands of Laertes and Horatio, and commands them to unite their virtues (as a coalition of ministers) to " calm the troubled land." The old couplet as to the bodies concludes the play.

Whichever of these two accounts is right, one thing at least is self-evident, Garrick has sadly mangled Shakespeare's play. We can detect the application of some of the dramatic principles so dear to the classicists. The violation of the unities is made somewhat less pronounced through the omission of young Fortinbras or at least his return; the gravediggers disappear because their jocularity was regarded as incongruous with the tragic affairs amongst which it is placed; the character of Laertes is elevated to make him such a model of virtue as a true hero should be; and Osric is removed perhaps for the same reason as the gravediggers, or perhaps because it was regarded as against all rules to introduce a new character near the end of a play. Garrick, in his anxiety to get rid of the gravediggers, forgot to give poor Ophelia a Christian or any other burial, thus showing his failure to have a thorough command of all the action of the play, as well as thereby depriving us of many of the fine lines and passages of the original. Whichever way Garrick made the King meet his death, Shakespeare has handled the matter more according to the villain's desert. The Queen's dying behind the scenes was doubtless a concession to the feeling that it was not good taste that a woman's violent death should be witnessed by the audience. If Laertes was left alive, it was to take the place of the omitted Fortinbras as the ruler of the kingdom. Although it is uncommon to bring on a character at the end of a play, we feel that Shakespeare was, however, artistic in having the affairs of the troubled kingdom pass into the hands of a valiant and virtuous foreign prince such as the young Norwegian shows himself to be.

We are pleased to learn that the theatre-goers of the day, who were beginning to tire of the continual presentation of Shakespeare in adulterated form, were not very favorably disposed towards this version, not even the acting of Garrick being able to make them take kindly to it. It was not often played, and after the revival of the original in 1780 was no more heard of. The day of Shakespeare alteration was nearing its end and few serious original attempts to correct the great Elizabethan were made after this date. Even if he were lacking in art as the playwrights and critics declared, the people began to prefer Shakespeare with all his imperfections on his head rather than with amendments.

Tate Wilkinson, manager of the theatres at Hull and York, who published in 1790 his memoirs, which are full of entertaining and valuable information as to the London and Dublin theatres, applied to Victor for a copy of Garrick's "Hamlet" as acted at Drury Lane. Victor in his reply said: "It is not in my power to send you the corrections lately made in 'Hamlet'; no such favor can be granted to anyone. I presume the play will never be printed with the alterations, as they are far from being universally liked; nay, they are greatly disliked by the million, who love Shakespeare with all his glorious absurdities and will not suffer a bold intruder to cut him up." This led Wilkinson to make an alteration himself, which he published in his "Wandering Patentee," a history of the Yorkshire theatres in four volumes, 1795. Genest thus describes it: "He [Wilkinson] divides the acts much as Garrick had done. In the Fifth Act, Hamlet fights with the King and kills him; the Queen runs out shrieking; Laertes kills Hamlet, but is not killed himself. Wilkinson, in professed imitation of Colley Cibber, that great improver of Shakespeare, inserts passages from some of his other plays, in particular, the fine scene of Cardinal Beaufort's death (the King speaks what belongs to the Cardinal)." That Wilkinson left Laertes alive makes it more probable that Boaden's account of Garrick's version is the correct one, for the later reviser would be influenced by his memory of his predecessor's procedure in this respect.

King Lear

The version of this most tragic of tragedies made by Nahum Tate, poet laureate and friend of Dryden, competes with Cibber's "Richard III" for the doubtful honor of being the most famous of the alterations of Shakespeare. "King Lear" was, as Downes testifies, acted after the Restoration as originally written, but, as it was considered too gloomy and terrible by the playgoers, Tate, as Lamb expresses it, "put his hook into the nostrils of this leviathan" in order that the actors might "draw the mighty beast about more easily." His version appeared in 1681. It superseded the original and in its own form, or as amended by Garrick, who put in more Shakespeare, and Kemble, who went back again to Tate, rejecting most of Garrick's restorations, kept the stage for nearly 160 years. Indeed, Shakespeare's play was so little known that managers did not hesitate to advertise the revisions of Tate as Shakespeare's play, and when the latter was revived in 1838 it was supposed by most of the audience to be an alteration.

Lamb has declared that "'Lear' is essentially impossible to be represented on a stage," because of its sublime tragic force, any adequate conception of which actors and stage machinery are impotent to give. This opinion, which seems to have won general acceptance, — "King Lear" is now rarely acted — partly exonerates Tate for his experiment, but is not meant to approve of the bungling manner in which he altered the play in the effort to make it more palatable to the theatre patrons of his time. As Tate has taken pains to set forth his attitude and purpose in his dedication, it is well to let him speak for himself. After declaring that nothing but the power of the persuasions of his friend [the person to whom his version is dedicated] and his own zeal for all the remains of Shakespeare could have impelled him to so bold an undertaking, he continues: "I found that the new-modelling of this story would force me sometimes on the difficult task of making the chiefest persons speak something like their character, on matter whereof I had no ground in my author. Lear's real and Edgar's pretended madness have so much of extravagant nature (I know not how else to express it) as could never have started but from our Shakespeare's creating fancy. The images and language are so odd and surprising, and yet so agreeable and proper, that whilst we grant that none but Shakespeare could have formed such conceptions, yet we are satisfied that they were the only things in the world that ought to be said on those occasions. I found the whole . . . a heap of jewels, unstrung and unpolished; yet so dazzling in their disorder that I soon perceived I had seized a treasure. 'Twas my good fortune to light on one expedient to rectify what was wanting in the regularity and probability of the tale, which was to run through the whole, as love betwixt Edgar and Cordelia, that never changed a word with each other in the original. This renders Cordelia's indifference and her father's passion in the first scene probable. It likewise gives countenance to Edgar's disguise, making that a generous design that was before a poor shift to save his life. The distress of the story is evidently heightened by it; and it particularly gave occasion of a new scene or two of more success (perhaps) than merit. This method necessarily threw me on making the tale conclude in a success to the innocent distressed persons; otherwise I must have encumbered the stage with dead bodies, which conduct makes many tragedies conclude with unseasonable jests. Yet I was racked with no small fears for so bold a change, till I found it well received by my audience; and if this will not satisfy the reader, I can produce an authority that questionless will." He then quotes some remarks made by Dryden in the preface to his "Spanish Friar" as to the difficulty of making a tragedy end happily and the necessity of a writer's exercising art and judgment in order to do it without violence to probability. "I have one thing more to apologize for," Tate continues, "which is, that I have used less quaintness [refinement] of expression even in the newest parts of the play. I confess, 'twas design in me, partly to comply with my author's style, to make the scenes of a piece, and partly to give it some resemblance of the time and persons here represented."

My account of the play is drawn from a full description given in the New Variorum "King Lear."

The Fool is omitted, in obedience to the rule that comic and tragic should not be mingled, and the King of France also is, of course, rejected, as Cordelia is to have a different husband. At the opening of the play, Gloucester is already convinced of Edgar's treachery and Edmund is in high favor. As the royal procession is entering, before the division of the kingdom, Edgar declares to Cordelia his love for her. She assures him that his love is ardently returned, and her blunt answers to her father are represented as prompted, not so much by detestation of her sister's hypocrisy as by a desire to escape marriage with Burgundy. After she is cast off by her father and refused by Burgundy, Edgar renews his suit, but Cordelia, as would be proper for any fashionable young lady of Tate's time to do, becomes coquettish, thinking she must test Edgar's love by affected coldness. The forged letter is shown to Gloucester, after Edmund has persuaded Edgar to conceal himself. The rest of the First Act follows fairly closely the original.

In the Second Act, Edmund induces Edgar to fly and the angry Gloucester tells the former to pursue the fugitive and bring him "piecemeal" back. In the third scene, Edgar's soliloquy has an addition referring to his love for Cordelia and declaring that the hope of doing service to Cordelia in some "white minute" makes him want to live. The act does not depart widely from Shakespeare as to the conduct of the action.

The first scene of Act III is Act III, 2, of the original, without much change. In the next scene, Edmund receives letters from both Regan and Goneril, and to him enters Gloucester, who reveals that he is plotting to restore Lear. As the Earl goes out, Cordelia meets him and implores him to aid her father. Before he leaves her, he tells her of his plot to restore the king. Cordelia orders her maid, Arante, to provide her a disguise, as she is going to relieve her father in spite of her wicked sisters' decree of death to any that do so. Edmund, who has been standing meanwhile at a distance, and has overheard this, at first, in admiration of Cordelia, expresses a desire for her, which "hopeless fire" he says he must quench, but, later, determines to take advantage of his knowledge of her design to forward his own by sending two ruffians to seize her in some desert place. The next scene is Shakespeare's III, 4, the Fool's part, of course, being omitted. After Lear, Kent, and the others have departed, Cordelia and Arante enter, followed by Edmund's two ruffians, who seize them. The "white minute" Edgar has been hoping for has come; he rushes in with "Avaunt ye bloodhounds!" and drives them off (bawling "The devil, the devil!") with his quarter-staff. After keeping up his disguise for a short time, his great love is too much for him and he reveals his identity to her, whom he had recognized, and explains why he is disguised, not forgetting to refer to her injunction not to mention his love to her again. This overcomes her and she receives him most rapturously, declaring that his rags are dearer to her than a monarch's richest pomp. The scene ends with his offer to protect Cordelia and her maid, who must spend the night in the hovel. The next scene is that in which Gloucester's eyes are put out. At the close, the Earl utters a long speech lamenting the loss of his sight and expressing his purpose to seek revenge by gaining for the King and himself the pity of the people, to whom he proposes to exhibit himself for the purpose. When his revenge is accomplished, he will throw himself from some precipice.

From this point on, Tate departs more widely from Shakespeare.

At the opening of the Fourth Act, Edmund and Regan are seated in loverlike fashion, listening to music. After an exchange of mutual vows, Edmund, as he is about to depart, pulls out his picture, which he gives to Regan, and in so doing drops Goneril's note, thereby confirming Regan's jealousy. An officer then enters and announces a great rebellion stirred up by Gloucester. In the next scene, Edgar and Gloucester on their way to Dover are met by Kent and Cordelia, the latter of whom expresses to Gloucester her sorrow at being, even remotely, the cause of his misfortune. He forgives her and gives her his blessing. Kent, who is urged to assume the leadership of the rebellion, leaves for that purpose with Cordelia. The next scene is IV, 6, in which Tate adheres to the original pretty closely. Shakespeare's IV, 7, with little change, comes next. Lear's speech beginning "Be your tears wet?" is expanded to eight lines and otherwise altered, and the Doctor's speech is modified and given to the "Gentleman." After Lear is led off, Cordelia has a soliloquy which merits quotation as a sample of Tate's imitation of Shakespeare's style:

> "The gods restore you. — Hark I hear afar
> The beaten drum; old Kent's a man of 's word.
> O for an arm
> Like the fierce Thunderer's, when the earth-born sons
> Storm'd Heav'n, to fight this injur'd father's battle!
> That I cou'd shift my sex, and dye me deep
> In his opposer's blood! But as I may,
> With women's weapons, piety and pray'rs,
> I'll aid his cause. — You never-erring gods

Fight on his side, and thunder on his foes
Such tempests as his poor ag'd head sustain'd;
Your image suffers when a monarch bleeds.
'Tis your own cause, for that your succours bring.
Revenge yourselves and right an injur'd king."

The Fifth Act is, as the new conclusion necessitates, practically rewritten. It opens with a short scene between Goneril and her " Poisoner," in which the latter assures her that the banquet and poison for Regan are ready. In the next scene, Edmund, alone in his tent, exults, in rather too highly impassioned language for modern taste, over the success of his amours with the two sisters. In the third scene, after Edgar has left Gloucester to go into the battle, the Earl utters a soliloquy of some fifteen lines of turgid and tedious verse, regretting his inability to take part in the fray. Edgar returns with the news that the battle is lost, and Albany, Goneril, and others enter with Lear and Cordelia as prisoners. Goneril tells a captain, aside, to dispatch the prisoners. Then Edgar, in disguise, comes in, impeaches Edmund of treason, and challenges him. Kent, Cordelia, and Lear are left guarded, while the others depart to witness the duel. Lear expresses deepest regret that Kent and Cordelia, whom he had wronged, are witnesses of his disgrace and, worst of all, fellow-sufferers with him. He weeps and almost faints when told of Kent's following him as a servant. On recovery, he tells the guards to take them to prison, where he says they will " die the wonders of the world." The duel between Edgar and Edmund takes place after much boasting, respectively, of their legitimate and illegitimate births. Goneril and Regan avow their love and jealousy over Edmund's wounded body. Goneril then reveals to Regan that she has given her poison at the banquet on the previous evening, whereupon Regan informs her, with equal malignity, that she has done the same to her at her own banquet. Edmund stops their "untimely strife," as he calls it, and is borne out in resignation, sustained by the reflection:

> "Who would not choose, like me, to yield his breath
> T'have rival queens contend for him in death."

At the opening of the last scene, which is at the prison, Lear is asleep with his head in Cordelia's lap. She wonders what has become of Edgar. A captain and officers enter with ropes to hang the prisoners. Cordelia begs them, if they will not spare her father, at least to dispatch her first. They assent to her request, and are seizing her, when Lear charges them to spare her and, finding they have no pity, snatches a partisan and strikes two of them down. The rest leave Cordelia and turn on him. At this point Edgar and Albany enter, and the latter orders guards to seize "those instruments of cruelty." Cordelia exclaims, "My Edgar, Oh!" and he replies, "My dear Cordelia!" saying further that their sufferings are over. Albany has Kent brought in and has Edgar go out to guide his father in that he may hear the conclusion. Lear expects still to be killed and asks mercy for Cordelia. Albany assures him that blessings are coming to him, tells him of the wickedness of Goneril and Regan, and of Edmund's being mortally wounded, and informs him that he has resolved to restore the kingdom to him. Lear is greatly astonished and, after saying rapturously to Kent "Old Lear shall be a king again," adds "Cordelia then shall be a queen — Cordelia is a queen." Edgar enters with Gloucester, the latter of whom kneels to Lear and is told by the king to kneel to Cordelia, who has the sovereignty and is the queen. After Edgar tells Lear that Edmund, Goneril, and Regan are dead, Lear bids him take the crowned Cordelia. Gloucester, at the command of Lear, joins him in blessing them. Edgar and Cordelia modestly declare they are over-recompensed for their merit and sufferings. Lear proposes that Gloucester, Kent, and he retire to "some close cell" where they will pass the remainder of their days in " calm reflections " on their past fortunes, "cheered with relation of the prosperous reign of this celestial pair." Edgar ends the play with a speech on the happy outcome of things, concluding with the moral of it all:

> " Our drooping country now erects her head,
> Peace spreads her balmy wings, and Plenty blooms.
> Divine Cordelia, all the gods can witness
> How much thy love to empire I prefer!
> Thy bright example shall convince the world
> (Whatever storms of fortune are decreed)
> That Truth and Virtue shall at last succeed."

Such is the "King Lear" which delighted the audiences of the eighteenth century and in which Betterton and other great actors won applause! This is the "heap of jewels" when they have been strung and polished and their "disorder" has been removed!

Tate must have felt pleased and flattered indeed at the success of his "bold undertaking." For many years his version was accepted almost without question. The general opinion of it will appear from the criticism of Doctor Johnson on the play, who, in commenting on Shakespeare's treatment of Cordelia, says: "Shakespeare has suffered the virtue of Cordelia to perish in a just cause, contrary to the natural ideas of justice, to the hope of the reader, and, what is yet more strange, to the faith of the chronicles. A play in which the wicked prosper, and the virtuous miscarry, may doubtless be good, because it is a just representation of the common events of human life; but, since all reasonable beings naturally love justice, I cannot easily be persuaded that the observation of justice makes a play worse; or that, if other excellences are equal, the audience will not always rise better pleased from the final triumph of persecuted virtue. In the present case the public has decided. Cordelia, from the time of Tate, has always retired with victory and felicity. And, if my sensations could add anything to the general suffrage, I might relate, that I was many years ago so shocked by Cordelia's death, that I know not whether I ever endured to read again the last scenes of the play till I undertook to revise them as an editor."

Again, Arthur Murphy, whom Doctor Johnson pronounced a judicious critic, after saying, in the course of some remarks on this version, that he should like to see the experiment made of having Lear die as in the original, expresses his conviction " that the play, as it is altered, will always be most agreeable to an audience, as the circumstances of Lear's restoration, and the virtuous Edgar's alliance with the amiable Cordelia, must always call forth those gushing tears which are swelled and ennobled by a virtuous joy."

Our admiration for Addison is increased when we find him, in 1711, venturing to express his dissent from the then apparently universal opinion in the following words, "'King Lear' is an admirable tragedy — as Shakespeare wrote it; but, as it is reformed according to the chimerical notion of poetical justice, in my humble opinion it has lost half its beauty."

It will not be profitable to take time and space to do more than comment briefly on the principal changes in the plot, the love affair between Edgar and Cordelia, and the happy ending. The former, on which Tate especially prided himself, is chiefly to be condemned because it is unnecessary. Cordelia's behavior toward her father is most probable and natural as it is in Shakespeare. It does not need to be explained by the added motive of a desire to escape marriage to a suitor she does not love in order to marry Edgar. Further, Edgar's assumption of disguise to save his life is a good and sufficient reason for such a move. This new feature is really due to the influence of that notion, the baneful effect of which we have so often observed potent in the revision of Shakespeare, that the passion of love should be a prominent element in every play. It is responsible also for the amplification of Edmund's intrigues with Goneril and Regan. Shakespeare's purpose in this play is to show the results of yielding to various evil passions or weaknesses, anger, rashness, incontinency, ingratitude, etc., and to teach us to control or not to harbor them by letting us see the severe punishments that befell some persons who did yield to them. To make the outcome more tragic, he involves the innocent Cordelia in her erring father's fate. This he was perfectly justified in doing, and it is absolutely true to life. With a few inimitable touches he has made Cordelia one of the finest portrayals of the virtuous female character in literature, and that without bringing her much on the scene. Tate's Cordelia is far inferior, in spite of her greater prominence, and especially displeasing is his making her for a time a coquette.

Nor has he improved the characterizations of the wicked persons of the drama. Edmund, Goneril, and Regan are detestable enough in Shakespeare. Tate has unnecessarily made them even more villainous and unnatural.

The change in the dénouement of the play, by which it is converted into a tragi-comedy and robbed of most of its pathos, a change which met with such hearty approval for so many years, has been so well criticised by Lamb, that his comment on it may be said to be the final word, and as such I quote it: "A happy ending! As if the living martyrdom that Lear had gone through, — the flaying of his feelings alive, — did not make a fair dismissal from the stage of life the only decorous thing for him. If he is to live and be happy after, if he could sustain this world's burden after, why all this pudder and preparation, — why torment us with all this unnecessary sympathy? As if the childish pleasure of getting his gilt robes and sceptre again could tempt him to act over again his misused station, — as if at his years and with his experience, anything was left but to die."

I have already given a few examples of Tate's lame attempts to be Shakespearean. One or two others are so amusing from their bombastic character as to be worth quoting. When Gloucester says to Edmund in Act I, scene 2, "Wind me into him," Tate adds this choice bit of bloodthirstiness,

"That I may bite the traitor's heart, and fold
His bleeding entrails on my vengeful arm."

Again, in Act II, 4, when Regan asks, "What need one?" Lear is made to reply, instead of "O, reason not the need," etc. :

"Blood! Fire! here — leprosies and bluest plagues!
Room, room for hell to belch her horrors up
And drench the Circes in a stream of fire.
Hark how th' infernals echo to my rage
Their whips and snakes."

Regan comments, "How lewd a thing is passion!" and Goneril adds, "So old and stomachful!"

It was not until 1756 that any attempt was made to provide a different "King Lear" from Tate's. Garrick, in this year, wishing to produce the play and being not entirely satisfied with Tate's treatment of it, decided to reform Tate's version, by restoring some of the omitted portions of the original, rather than to go back to the latter entirely. Although he deserves some credit for the restorations, he is to be condemned for not venturing to discard Tate altogether. But he had to please his audiences, and it is charitable to believe that he felt compelled for commercial reasons to conform to their desires in respect to the retention of the love affair between Edgar and Cordelia. As might be expected of the man who omitted the gravediggers from "Hamlet," Garrick follows Tate in rejecting the Fool. He borrows from Tate in many minor respects, even when restoring Shakespeare, as in Edgar's soliloquy (II, 3) and in the second heath scene (III, 2). In his III, 1, he introduces lines from the scene between Cordelia and Gloucester in Tate. In scene 2, he retains the seizing of Cordelia and her maid by the two ruffians and her rescue by Edgar. Scene 3 is all Tate, as is IV, 1, and IV, 2. IV, 3, is Shakespeare's. The Fifth Act is practically all Tate's.

In 1768, the elder Colman brought out a version of "King Lear" at Covent Garden. Aside from omitting the Fool and making some transpositions and lesser omissions, Colman restored the first four acts of Shakespeare. The Fifth Act is however largely taken from Tate, although he rejected the love affair between Edgar and Cordelia. His alteration was not well received and was soon withdrawn. The audience were displeased at being deprived of the love scenes.

Colman, in his advertisement, makes some judicious remarks on Tate's version that are worth giving as a part of the criticism of it: "This very expedient," he says, "of a love between Edgar and Cordelia, on which Tate felicitates himself, seemed to me to be one of the capital objections to his alteration. For even supposing that it rendered Cordelia's indifference to her father more probable (an indifference which Shakespeare has nowhere implied), it assigns a very poor motive for it; so that what Edgar gains on the side of romantic generosity, Cordelia loses on that of real virtue. Tate, in whose days love was the soul of tragedy as well as comedy, was, however, so devoted to intrigue that he has not only given Edmund a passion for Cordelia, but has injudiciously amplified on his criminal commerce with Goneril and Regan, which is the most disgusting part of the original. In all these circumstances, it is generally agreed, that Tate's alteration is for the worse; and his 'King Lear' would probably have quitted the stage long ago had he not made 'the tale conclude in a success to the innocent distressed persons.' Even in this catastrophe, he has incurred the censure of Addison, but 'in the present case,' says Doctor Johnson, 'the public has decided, and Cordelia, from the time of Tate, has always retired with victory and felicity.'

"To reconcile the catastrophe of Tate to the story of Shakespeare, was the first grand object which I proposed to myself in this alteration, . . . and I have now endeavored to purge the tragedy of 'Lear' of the alloy of Tate, which has so long been suffered to debase it."

He goes on to criticise some of the features of Shakespeare's play that seemed to him not consistent with nature and which he therefore removed when possible: "The utter improbability of Gloster's imagining, though blind, that he had leaped down Dover Cliff, has been justly censured by Doctor Warton; and in the representation it is still more liable to objection than in print. I have, therefore, without scruple, omitted it, preserving, however, at the same time, that celebrated description of the cliff in the mouth of Edgar. The putting out Gloster's eyes is also so unpleasing a circumstance, that I would have altered it, if possible, but, upon examination, it appeared to be so closely interwoven with the fable, that I durst not venture to change it. I had once some idea of retaining the character of the Fool; but, though Doctor Warton has very truly observed that the poet 'has so well conducted even the natural jargon of the Beggar and the jestings of the Fool, which in other hands must have sunk into burlesque, that they contribute to heighten the pathetic'; yet, after the most serious consideration, I was convinced that such a scene 'would sink into burlesque' in the representation, and would not be endured on the modern stage."

We believe his and Warton's opinion as to the cliff episode erroneous, for it is perfectly natural that a blind, superstitious, credulous, and distracted old man, such as Gloucester was, should imagine almost anything to have happened to him. We think also that the Fool should be retained, if the cast includes an actor capable of doing the part justice.

172 ALTERATIONS AND ADAPTATIONS

Garrick's alteration held the stage for fifty years. In 1809, Kemble saw fit to try his hand on the play. There was no reason for him to touch it unless he intended to restore more of Shakespeare; but this was far from his purpose. Instead of restoring more of Shakespeare, he, to his everlasting disgrace, restored more of Tate. Indeed, Shakespeare and Tate were treated with no discrimination by him. He is said even to have advertised his "King Lear" as Shakespeare's play.

Kemble begins his play like Tate and to him the First Act adheres closely. One of Kemble's own additions is a direction for Oswald to enter singing "tol de rol," etc. Acts II and III are virtually Tate's, some that Garrick had rejected in the latter being restored. Act IV begins with the last scene of Tate's Act III. Kemble omits Gloucester's soliloquy, his fall from the cliff, and the most essential part of Oswald's dying speech (which Garrick had restored). His Fifth Act does not differ greatly from Garrick's. More of Tate however is restored. This alteration, which is thus seen to be far worse than Garrick's, is a great blot on Kemble's reputation as a man of taste in dramatic matters and a marked manifestation of his lack of reverence for Shakespeare.

In "King Lear" as produced by Kean in 1824 at the Theatre Royal, the first four acts follow Tate closely, with occasional restorations of lines from Shakespeare. The Fifth Act has for its first scene the last scene of Tate's Act IV. Scene 2 is Shakespeare's. Scene 3 is in the main like Shakespeare, but some of Gloucester's soliloquy from Tate is introduced.

Othello, the Moor of Venice
This play has happily escaped alteration.

CHAPTER IX. ANTONY AND CLEOPATRA — CYMBELINE — PERICLES

Antony and Cleopatra

THIS play was fitted for the stage by Edward Capell, the Shakespeare editor, and acted at Drury Lane, January 3, 1759, with Garrick, who supervised the production, as Antony. The adaptation was merely by transposition of scenes and abridgment. For convenience of representation a number of the minor characters were omitted, but their speeches were in many cases transferred, often without propriety, to other characters. A stanza was added to the drinking song in II, 7.

Dryden's dramatic masterpiece "All for Love" is not an alteration of Shakespeare, but a new play, professedly in imitation of him, on the same subject. Sir Charles Sedley also wrote a play, in rime, with the title of "Antony and Cleopatra," but it is entirely independent of Shakespeare's drama.

In 1813, "Antony and Cleopatra" was revived at Covent Garden, with additions from Dryden. This alteration was probably made by Kemble. The play follows Shakespeare fairly closely as far as II, 4, though with many unnecessary changes of words. The rest of the Second Act is mostly from Dryden. After Antony's entrance, the scene in Dryden's Act II, in which Antony and Cleopatra reproach each other, is introduced with slight changes. Genest says of this: " Dryden's scene is a very good one, but it is not introduced in this place with propriety. In Dryden's play, Ventidius in the First Act estranges Antony from Cleopatra, after which, naturally, follows the scene in which Antony reproaches her; but the editor of the present play reverses the order of things and makes Dryden's second scene precede his first. In Dryden's play, the scene lies the whole time at Alexandria, but in this alteration Antony is represented as coming back to Egypt merely to tell Cleopatra that they must part, which is not only contrary to the fact, but absurd in itself. There was nothing like a quarrel between Antony and Cleopatra till after the battle of Actium."

Act III, which begins with Shakespeare's III, 6, follows him, with slight changes. The sea fight is represented before the audience in a scene without dialogue.

Act IV is almost wholly Dryden's. The scene between Antony and Ventidius from Dryden's Third Act, in which Ventidius exhorts Antony to continue warring against Cæsar, is inserted. Dolabella enters and to him Antony describes Cleopatra on the Cydnus, partly in the lines of Shakespeare and partly in those of Dryden. Dolabella announces conditions from Cæsar. Then comes the scene from Dryden between Antony and Octavia, which should have been left out, as it takes the place of Shakespearean scenes of greater merit. Moreover, Octavia's coming to Antony in Egypt is an unnecessary poetical fiction.

The Fifth Act is a combination of Shakespeare and Dryden. As in Dryden, Ventidius kills himself when asked by Antony to kill him, and thus shames Antony into falling on his sword. Before Antony dies, he is taken to Cleopatra and the scene between them is, with much abridgment, like Shakespeare. A short scene is introduced between Proculeius and

Dolabella, in which the latter mourns for Antony and says that Antony's adherents will attend to the funeral arrangements. The play then ends with a grand funeral procession with epicedium. Many of Dryden's lines are used in this scene. The practice of amalgamating plays of two authors has already been sufficiently discussed in other connections. It may be said of this, that it is perhaps the best of such combinations, for the reason that the editor has in the main chosen the best parts of Dryden's play and has refrained from inserting in the patchwork, matter of his own invention. However, there was plenty of material in Shakespeare's play and consequently no necessity to borrow from Dryden.

Cymbeline

Cymbeline, which is really a tragi-comedy, although placed among the tragedies by the First Folio editors, was first altered as early as 1682 by "Tom" Durfey, the favorite entertainer of the "Merry Monarch" and his successors, and the author of numerous dramas and other works. Durfey made material changes both as to the plot and the language. He also altered the title and the names, descriptions, etc., of several of the characters. On the title page of the copy of the play I have seen, the title is given as "The Injured Princess, or the Fatal Wager," but, curiously enough, on the first page and at the top of all the pages of the play it appears as "The Unequal Match, or the Fatal Wager." As might be expected, the scenes in Italy are transferred to France. The new play is decidedly Frenchified.

Shakespeare's Iachimo becomes Shatillion, an opinionated Frenchman, and the Iachimo of this play

176 ALTERATIONS AND ADAPTATIONS

is a "roaring drunken lord," a companion of Cloten.
Posthumus is renamed Ursaces, and Imogen, Eugenia.
Pisanio is turned into a lord and made the father of
Clarinna, a new character, the confidante of Eugenia.
The part of Guiderius is transferred to Arviragus,
and the other young prince is called Palladour.

The first scene of the First Act begins with the
parting of Ursaces and Eugenia (only a few lines
from Shakespeare) and continues with some dialogue
between Cymbeline, Eugenia, and Ursaces (somewhat
like Shakespeare's), and with the dialogue
between Cloten and his companions (a very little
from Shakespeare's scene 2), and ends with some
dialogue between the Queen and her women, in which
she inquires if the doctor has come and speaks of
Eugenia's voluntary seclusion of herself from everybody
but Clarinna. Scene 2 is Shakespeare's I, 4, but
laid in France. Durfey follows the original more
closely in this scene than in any other.

Act II, scene 1, is mostly new, and at first Cymbeline,
the Queen, Pisanio, and the Doctor are the
participants. They talk of Eugenia's conduct (a
few words only from II, 3), and Cymbeline and the
Queen blame Pisanio for favoring Ursaces. After
the King and Pisanio retire, the remainder of the
scene is somewhat like I, 5. Scene 2 is I, 6, with the
dialogue greatly altered and much additional. Scene
3 is entirely new. The Queen gives Pisanio the vial,
the contents of which she tells him are a sure cure for
disease, as an earnest of future favor. After she
departs, Pisanio shows in a soliloquy that he suspects
her. Scene 4 has first a part like II, 1, and then a
part a little like II, 3 (up to "Enter Cymbeline and
Queen").

Act III, scene 1 is II, 4, and scene 2 is II, 5, of

course much changed. Scene 3 is made up of II, 3, III, 2, and III, 4, very much altered. Pisanio believes Eugenia false to Ursaces but spares her life and gives her the vial he had received from the Queen. Eugenia has a soliloquy at the end of the act. In the First Scene of the Fourth Act, the Queen scolds Clarinna for concealing Eugenia's escape and commands Iachimo to punish her. The King enters and orders a thorough search to be made for Eugenia, and then a captain comes in and informs Cymbeline of the landing of the Roman army. Scene 2 is in the main like III, 6, a great deal altered both in Eugenia's soliloquy and in the remainder. In Scene 3, Cloten, disguised as Ursaces, enters with Iachimo, dragging in Clarinna. On Iachimo's attempting to ravish her, she cries for help and her father, who is near by, appears on the scene. Clarinna flees and Pisanio fights with Iachimo and kills him. Thereupon Cloten puts out Pisanio's eyes, after which he goes in quest of Clarinna. Scene 4 is at first a little like IV, 2, and then follows a part in which Bellario and the two princes decide to fight for the King.

Act V, scene 1 is the soliloquy of Ursaces, altered much for the worse. Durfey adds a contemporary touch which is remarkably out of place in this play and which is worth quoting as an example of the depraved dramatic taste of the author and of his time, and as an indication of the low moral tone then prevalent. Ursaces says that if every woman that forfeits honor should be deprived of life,

> " The full-fed city dame would sin in fear;
> The divine's daughter slight the amorous cringe
> Of her tall lover; the close salacious Puritan
> Forget th' appointment with her canting brother."

Scene 2 is the battle scene, mostly the work of Durfey. Eugenia is present and recognizes Shatillion, who is disguised as a Briton. Ursaces kills him after he has acknowledged Eugenia's innocence, and is about to take his own life, when he is seized and taken to the King. In scene 3, the dénouement takes place, much as in Shakespeare's V, 5, but the scene is greatly shortened.

As an alteration of Shakespeare this is wretched, but Durfey's additions, considered by themselves, are by no means wholly despicable. In the epilogue he calls the play a comedy, yet it is more tragic than "Cymbeline."

It would be useless and tedious to do more than comment on a few of the principal features of this version. The greatest change in the plot made by Durfey is that which is shown in the second scene of Act V, namely, the killing by Ursaces of the destroyer of his peace of mind. In no instance is the genius and higher purpose of Shakespeare more clearly to be seen. Durfey's rather ordinary dramatic instincts led him to punish Shatillion (Iachimo) as a sort of poetical justice, and thus to detract from the characterization of Ursaces (Posthumus); whereas Shakespeare's supreme dramatic ability made him make of his hero a rare exponent of magnanimity, a man who, perceiving that he himself had erred, was ready to forgive another as he had been forgiven. How much higher a justice this than the so-called poetical justice of the classicists! This is only another of the many lamentable failures of lesser minds to improve upon Shakespeare.

Nothing can be said in favor of the addition of Clarinna and the scenes in which she figures. It is an unnecessary one and therefore bad. The third scene of Act IV, the scene which has most to do with her affairs, is especially unwelcome because of its moral and physical unpleasantness, both occasioned by the taste and character of Durfey and his time. Although enough of the original plot has been retained to prevent the play from being very bad as a play of Durfey's, yet from the point of view of its relationship to its original, it is highly censurable, like most other similar revisions of Shakespeare, in that too much of the alterer's own has been substituted for better material, and in that, what is still more blameworthy, the diction of the parts that are retained has been treated in such a way as to remove or disguise most of its beauties.

Another alteration of "Cymbeline" was made by Charles Marsh, whom we have met before as a reviser of "The Winter's Tale," in 1755. Marsh's play was not acted and, although it was printed, I have not seen a copy of it. The following quotation from the "Biographia Dramatica" is all I have found concerning it: "Though Mr. Marsh was not at that time a magistrate, the dullness he displayed in the present undertaking, afforded strong presumptions of his future rise to a seat on the bench at Guildhall, Westminster."

A third and very material alteration was that produced in 1759 by William Hawkins, M. A., at one time Professor of Poetry in the University of Oxford. Hawkins had great difficulty in getting his play properly represented, a fact to which he refers in the dedication and preface, for Mrs. Bellamy declined the part of Imogen and the part of Philario was taken by an actor inadequate for it.

The reviser's spirit and method of treatment will best be made evident by letting his speak for himself:

"I have endeavored," he says in the preface, "to new-construct this tragedy almost upon the plan of Aristotle himself in respect to the unity of time; with so thorough a veneration however for the great father of the English stage that, even while I have presumed to regulate and modernize his design, I have thought it an honor to tread in his steps, and to imitate his style, with the humility and reverence of a son. With this view, I have retained in many places the very language of the original author, and in all others endeavored to supply it with a diction similar thereunto; so that, as an unknown friend of mine has observed, the present attempt is entirely new, whether it be considered as an alteration from or an imitation of Shakespeare." Accordingly, we find the unity of time observed and that of place more nearly adhered to, but the foregoing extract gives no conception of the violent changes in the plot that Hawkins made in his solicitude for regularity and in his presumption of trying to improve upon the original.

The character of Iachimo is rejected and the first part of that of Posthumus; Palador and Cadwall are the names of the two princes; the Queen is spoken of as lately dead; the Pisanio of the original becomes Philario and is made a friend, instead of a servant, to Posthumus; the Pisanio of this play is an Italian, a tool of Cloten's, who takes the place to some extent of Iachimo; Cloten is made a serious character; the parts of Palador and Philario are enlarged ("improved" says Hawkins).

The play opens at about Act II, 4, of the original, a little introductory matter however being added. Caius Lucius demands tribute of Cymbeline, which the latter refuses to pay; Cymbeline tells Cloten he has disinherited Imogen and made him his heir;

Pisanio tells Cloten by what arts he has imposed upon Posthumus and made him believe Imogen to be false; Imogen is discovered in prison; Philario persuades her to escape in the disguise of a boy.

In Act II, Cloten and Cymbeline discover that Imogen has fled (as in III, 5); then follow scene 3 of Act III, not much modified, and scene 4 of the same act, altered decidedly for the worse; then Bellarius returns and Philario and Imogen are kindly received by him.

In Act III, Philario, in a soliloquy, doubts the innocence of Imogen. When Bellarius enters he praises the two princes in a number of lines, several of which are from "Troilus and Cressida." Philario tells Imogen that the drug he has given her is poison. Then follows a part of IV, 2 (Cadwall sings a modified form of the dirge).

Act IV opens on the field of battle and is something like V, 2. Palador kills Pisanio, who, before he dies, gives him a note of Cloten's, which discloses their villainy and which he desires him to give to Posthumus. It is not told how Pisanio knew Posthumus to be in the battle, or how Palador was to find him, but Posthumus is made to come on the scene, with obliging opportuneness, and is thereupon convinced of his wife's innocence. Philario, who throughout the play is a very inconsistent character, when reproached by Posthumus for having been the instrument of his cruelty, refrains from revealing the fact that the Princess is alive. At this point, Cymbeline comes in and is requested to go to the cave.

In Act V, Palador, Cadwall, and Imogen are first disclosed; then Philario enters and, we cannot imagine for what reason, tells Imogen that her husband is dead; Cymbeline and others then appear and the play ends, as regards the action, much as in Shakespeare. Here indeed the pseudo-classic influence has produced a sad result, for a play of Shakespeare's has, in the effort to make it regular, been outrageously mutilated. For many of the changes there seems to be no discoverable reason aside from mere whimsicality. Much of the first portion of the play which throws light upon the characters and belongs to their development has most improperly been rejected. Shakespeare's Pisanio is spoiled in Hawkins's enlarged characterization of him under the name of Philario. As in Durfey, the conception of Posthumus, whom in general Hawkins has rendered less conspicuous, is much injured by depriving him of the opportunity to display his magnanimity and forgiving spirit. We fail to see wherein it improves the part of Palador to make him the instrument of the Hawkins Pisanio's punishment. Poetical justice is doubtless responsible for this procedure. The transformed Cloten as instigator of the attempt on Imogen, which is not undertaken for a wager but out of malice towards Posthumus, is far less natural than Shakespeare's Cloten, the base tool of an ambitious mother.

It would be wearisome and unprofitable to discuss the action of Hawkins's play. Suffice it to say that the whole development of the plot is managed with infinitely less art than in the original, and that the verse added bears no very striking resemblance to Shakespeare's diction, in spite of the compiler's avowed endeavor to imitate it. Of the later versions, this is about the most violent and most wretched. That such an alteration as this should be presented to the public so late as 1759 removes all wonder that the earlier revisers, at a time when Shakespeare was less in favor, should think themselves at liberty to mangle his dramas as they did. And in this instance the mutilation is, *mirabile dictu,* the work of a professor of poetry in the University of Oxford! Garrick's adaptation of "Cymbeline," which was first acted at Drury Lane, November 28, 1761, is in the main a most judicious one, for, this time, he was content to omit and transpose only what seemed necessary. In one respect a bad change was made, for the dirge, instead of being given as in Shakespeare, was sung as abridged from Hawkins.

Henry Brooke, author of "The Fool of Quality," also published a play with the title of "Cymbeline," which differs so much from Shakespeare's play that it cannot be called an alteration of it. Yet the outlines of Brooke's play are borrowed from his predecessor and he doubtless had Shakespeare before him as he wrote. The scene in Imogen's bedchamber (Shakespeare's II, 2) is the only scene (it is Brooke's II, 7) in which there is much direct borrowing. Practically the entire play is written afresh in a manner far inferior to Shakespeare.

Pericles

A portion, the last two acts, of this partly Shakespearean play was altered into a three-act drama by George Lillo, author of the first specimens of the bourgeois tragedy or modern melodrama. Lillo, who was a London jeweler and is chiefly remembered for his tragedy of "George Barnwell," admired Shakespeare, and had taste enough to recognize his work. The spirit in which he went to work at "Pericles" appears from his prologue, which I quote:

" Hard is the task, in this discerning age,
    To find new subjects that will bear the stage;

> And bold our bards, their low harsh strains to bring
> Where Avon's swan has long been heard to sing;
> Blest parent of our scene! whose matchless wit,
> Tho' yearly reap'd, is our best harvest yet.
> Well may that genius every heart command,
> Who drew all Nature with her own strong hand;
> As various, as harmonious, fair and great,
> With the same vigor and immortal heat;
> As thro' each element and form she shines:
> We view heav'n's handmaid in her Shakespeare's
>   lines,
> Though some mean scenes, injurious to his fame,
> Have long usurp'd the honor of his name;
> To glean and clear from chaff his least remains,
> Is just to him, and richly worth our pains.
> We dare not charge the whole unequal play
> Of Pericles on him; yet let us say,
> As gold tho' mix'd with baser metal shines,
> So do his bright inimitable lines
> Throughout those rude wild scenes distinguish'd
>   stand,
> And shew he touch'd them with no sparing hand."

He called his play "Marina," after the heroine, with whose story the portion he adapted deals. It was first acted, August 11, 1738, at Covent Garden. The dramatis personæ are altered somewhat and are: Pericles, King of Tyre; Lysimachus, Governor of Ephesus; Escanes, attendant on Pericles; Leonine, a young lord of Tharsus; Valdes, captain of a crew of pirates; Boult, a pander; Thaisa, Queen of Tyre; Philoten, Queen of Tharsus (she is the daughter of Cleon and Dionyza, who are omitted from "Marina," and is not a character in "Pericles," but in this play takes the place of her mother); Marina, daughter to Pericles and Thaisa; Mother Coupler, a bawd, etc. The scene is laid at Tharsus and Ephesus only.

The play begins with Philoten's instructions to Leonine to kill Marina and Marina's rescue by pirates ("Pericles" IV, 1). The pirates speak much more than in the old play. The Queen is represented as in love with Leonine. Scene 2 is the brothel scene considerably altered (dialogue is added from "Pericles" IV, 3).

The Second Act, in the first scene, has some lines like "Pericles" IV, 4. The Queen is represented as repentant and Leonine as claiming her as his reward. Then Pericles enters, speaks of Marina, is informed of her death (words from various parts of the original are used), and then laments before Marina's monument, the dumb show being thus turned into dialogue. The Queen refuses to wed Leonine, and he stabs her and is then seized by the guards. Scene 2 is a brothel scene ("Pericles" IV, 6). Marina is rescued by Lysimachus's officers instead of by Boult.

Act III, scene 1 consists of a dialogue of accusation and recrimination between Boult and Mother Coupler. In scene 2, at first, two priests, in the temple of Diana at Ephesus, are talking about Thaisa and they speak of her resemblance to Marina. Thaisa awakes, having dreamed of Pericles. Lysimachus enters and asks her if she has learned anything about the young maid he has intrusted to her. She replies in the negative. The ship of Pericles then appears and the king is brought in. Marina is led in to try to restore him. She tries singing and then tells her story (like "Pericles" V, 1). Her father recognizes her and Thaisa recognizes him, etc., as in the original (V, 3). Lysimachus is to have Marina for wife. There is no revenge as Leonine has already killed Philoten.

Lillo will thus be seen to have fallen short of real-izing the expectations that might have been formed from his prologue. He has omitted parts, as the scene between Cleon and Dionyza (IV, 3), which are far superior to his own indifferent additions. He has made a fairly good play, however, and we are not disposed to censure him highly for his performance, which, especially when compared with some others of the kind, is not altogether discreditable.

III
EPILOGUE

EPILOGUE

THE list and accounts of these dramatic perversions are now completed. Taken together, these alterations and adaptations will be seen to constitute a body of dramatic literature which is considerable, quantitatively, only two or three plays having escaped treatment of this kind. Happily, they have, however, been for the most part discarded and forgotten. "And thus the whirligig of time brings in his revenges." Shakespeare, whom they for a time crowded almost entirely from the scene, has, by the mere force of his genius, survived his temporary displacement, thereby proving conclusively, if proof were needed, that his works are "not for an age," as were those of his would-be improvers, "but for all time." That this change has been effected makes one have renewed confidence that the literary judgment of time is unerring. Now, these remodeled plays, once so important, have interest merely as literary curiosities and as manifestations of dramatic notions forever and rightfully rejected.

A word, in conclusion, as to the value of this investigation. Besides the knowledge it has afforded of the history of the stage and of the opinion as to Shakespeare, it has been, above all, of incalculable benefit in throwing light on Shakespeare as the supreme dramatic artist. In no way could the superiority of his dramatic methods, almost unfailingly exhibiting that fidelity to nature or trueness to life which constitutes genuine art, be more clearly manifested than by having them thus thrown into comparison with those employed by playwrights who, for the most part, were possessed of little talent or no genius for dramatic composition and who stultified themselves by attempting to deal with the same situations and to improve what they in their blindness believed to be inartistic.